The Ultimate Beginners Guide to Private Equity Real Estate Investing

Real Estate Investing, Volume 9

Jim Pellerin

Published by Jim Pellerin, 2023.

THE ULTIMATE BEGINNERS GUIDE TO PRIVATE EQUITY REAL ESTATE INVESTING

First edition. May 11, 2023.

Copyright © 2023 Jim Pellerin.

ISBN: 979-8223688594

Written by Jim Pellerin.

Also by Jim Pellerin

Real Estate Investing
Real Estate Investing Strategies: The Secret to Financial Independence with Real Estate
Real Estate Investing with Lease Options - Investing in Real Estate with No Money Down
Invest Now - The Passive Approach to Winning at Real Estate
The Ultimate Beginners Guide to Real Estate Investing
The 98 Best Real Estate Investing Strategies
The Ultimate Beginners Guide to Wholesale Real Estate Investing
The Ultimate Beginners Guide to Rental Real Estate Investing
The Ultimate Beginners Guide to Fix and Flip Real Estate Investing
The Ultimate Beginners Guide to Private Equity Real Estate Investing

Watch for more at www.jimpellerin.com.

Table of Contents

....1

Why You Should Read This Book.......................................3

Chapter 1: Introduction to Private Equity Real Estate Investing..........9

Chapter 2: How to Set Up a Private Equity Real Estate Investing Firm...23

Chapter 3: Financing Private Equity Real Estate Investments.............37

Chapter 4: What is the Private Equity Capital Stack?....................51

Chapter 5: Raising Capital for Private Equity Real Estate Funds.......61

Chapter 6: Evaluating Real Estate Investment Opportunities.............77

Chapter 7: Investing in Private Equity Residential Real Estate...........89

Chapter 8: Investing in Commercial Private Equity Real Estate......101

Chapter 9: Investing in Private Equity Real Estate Office Buildings...113

Chapter 10: Investing in Private Equity Real Estate Retail Buildings...125

Chapter 11: Investing in Private Equity Real Estate Industrial Buildings...137

Chapter 12: Investing in Private Equity Real Estate Hospitality Buildings...151

Chapter 13: Investing in Private Equity Real Estate Funds...............161

Chapter 14: Private Equity Crowdfunding............................173

Chapter 15: Understanding Real Estate Investment Trusts (REITs) 185

Chapter 16: Tax Considerations for Private Equity Real Estate Investing.. 197

About The Author 209

Other Books By Jim Pellerin 211

The Ultimate Beginners Guide to Private Equity Real Estate Investing

An Overiew of Private Equity

Real Estate Investing

Jim Pellerin

Updated for 2023

Why You Should Read This Book

Most people who want to get started with Real Estate Investing, have no idea how to get sarted. Or worse, they have some idea how to get started but it is the wrong strategy for them.

This book provides an overview of how to get started in Private Equity Real Estate Investing. This book is NOT a practical approach to Private Equity Real Estate Investing and the reader is NOT expected to be able to start a private equity firm/fund after completing this book.

In this book, you will learn enough information to be able to decide if Private Eqituity real estate investing is right for you.

Learning Method

This book is meant to teach you the information using special information presentation techniques. These techniques will enhance your learning and retention experience.

Most chapters are structured as follows:

1. Tell you what you are going to learn
2. Provide the learning information
3. Tell you what you just leanred

JIM PELLERIN

The Ultimate Beginners Guide to Private Equity Real Estate Investing

Chapter 1: Introduction to Private Equity Real Estate Investing

Photo by Markus Winkler

1.1 Understanding Private Equity Real Estate Investing

This section provides an overview of private equity real estate investing, including its definition, distinctions from publicly traded real estate investments, historical growth, and key advantages. Private equity real estate investing involves investing in real estate through private investment vehicles, such as private equity funds, and offers benefits such as higher returns, diversification, and greater control. Understanding these key aspects is crucial for investors considering private equity real estate as an investment option.

Private Equity Real Estate (PERE) investing refers to the practice of investing in **privately held real estate assets**, typically through a **pooled fund structure**. Unlike publicly traded real estate investments, such as real estate investment trusts (REITs) that can be bought and sold on stock exchanges, PERE investments involve *direct ownership* *of properties* or interests in real estate projects. This approach provides investors with the opportunity to participate in the real estate market's potential for capital appreciation and income generation.

One key distinction between publicly traded real estate investments (REITs) and PERE investments lies in the level of control and flexibility. Publicly traded investments are subject to market volatility and can be influenced by factors beyond an investor's control. In contrast, **PERE investors have more direct control** over their investments. They can carefully select properties or projects, conduct thorough due diligence, and negotiate terms and conditions that align with their investment objectives. This level of control allows PERE investors to have a more hands-on approach to managing their real estate investments.

Private equity real estate has experienced **significant growth** over the years, becoming a vital part of the overall real estate industry. This growth can be attributed to several factors:

1. Firstly, PERE investments offer **diversification benefits** by providing exposure to a different asset class within an investment portfolio. Real estate has historically exhibited low correlation with other financial assets, making it an attractive option for investors seeking to reduce overall portfolio risk.
2. Additionally, the potential for **long-term capital appreciation** and income generation from rental properties has made PERE investments appealing to both institutional and individual investors.

Investing in private equity real estate offers various advantages and benefits.

THE ULTIMATE BEGINNERS GUIDE TO PRIVATE EQUITY REAL ESTATE INVESTING

1. One significant advantage is the potential for **higher returns** compared to publicly traded real estate investments. Private equity real estate funds often target *value-add* or *opportunistic strategies*, which involve acquiring properties with the intention of improving them and generating higher returns upon sale. This active management approach can lead to enhanced returns through property *renovations*, *repositioning*, or *development projects*.

2. Another benefit of PERE investing is the potential for **consistent income** generation. Unlike stocks or bonds, which primarily generate income through dividends or coupon payments, real estate investments can provide a steady cash flow through *rental income*. This income stream can be particularly appealing to investors seeking stable and predictable cash flow to support their financial goals, such as *retirement planning*.

Furthermore, investing in private equity real estate allows investors to gain exposure to specific real estate sectors or geographic regions that may be difficult to access through other investment vehicles. PERE funds often specialize in specific property types, such as *office buildings*, *retail centers*, or *multifamily residential properties*. By investing in these funds, investors can benefit from the expertise and market knowledge of experienced real estate professionals who focus on a particular niche.

In conclusion, private equity real estate investing offers distinct advantages and benefits compared to publicly traded real estate investments. The control, flexibility, and potential for higher returns make PERE investments an attractive option for investors seeking to diversify their portfolios and capitalize on the income and growth potential of the real estate market. With its historical growth and increasing importance within the industry, private equity real estate has become a significant player in the global investment landscape.

1.2 Types of Private Equity Real Estate Investments

Private equity real estate investments encompass a variety of strategies that cater to different risk appetites and investment objectives. Understanding the different types of private equity real estate investments can help investors make informed decisions based on their goals and preferences.

One common type of private equity real estate investment is **core strategies**, which involve acquiring stable income-producing properties. These properties are typically well-established, fully leased, and generate *consistent rental income*. Core investments are considered *lower risk* and provide *steady cash flow* to investors. They often target properties in prime locations with strong tenant demand, such as Class A office buildings or high-quality retail centers. Core strategies are popular among institutional investors seeking long-term income and capital preservation.

Value-add strategies involve acquiring properties with the intention of adding value through *renovations, improvements,* or *repositioning.* These investments require *active management* and hands-on involvement to enhance the property's value and generate higher returns. Value-add opportunities may include *upgrading building systems, renovating units,* or *reconfiguring spaces* to attract higher-paying tenants. By implementing these improvements, investors aim to increase rental income and property value over time. Value-add investments offer potential for *higher returns* compared to core strategies but also entail *higher risk* due to the execution and market factors involved.

Opportunistic strategies represent a high-risk, high-reward approach to private equity real estate investing. These investments typically involve acquiring *underperforming* or *distressed properties* that require significant repositioning or development efforts. Opportunistic investors seek to capitalize on unique market conditions or specific situations that can lead to substantial value creation. Examples include purchasing vacant land for development, repositioning outdated properties in emerging markets, or capitalizing on distressed market cycles. These investments offer the potential for *significant returns* but are also subject to *higher uncertainty* and market volatility.

Distressed investing focuses on acquiring *financially troubled properties* or debt instruments tied to real estate assets. During economic downturns or market disruptions, distressed opportunities arise as property owners or borrowers face financial distress. Distressed investors aim to capitalize on these situations by acquiring properties or debt at *discounted prices* and then restructuring or repositioning them for *eventual profit*. Distressed investing requires specialized expertise in navigating complex legal and financial aspects, as well as the ability to manage and turn around troubled assets effectively.

Private equity real estate investments also offer opportunities to focus on specialized sectors or asset types. Investors can choose to target specific property types, such as **hospitality, healthcare, industrial**, or **residential** properties, based on their expertise or market insights. Specialized sector investments allow investors to leverage their knowledge and experience in a *particular niche*, potentially leading to enhanced returns and risk mitigation. For example, investing in the healthcare sector may involve acquiring medical office buildings or senior living facilities, taking advantage of demographic trends and the increasing demand for healthcare-related real estate.

In summary, private equity real estate investments encompass various strategies that cater to different risk profiles and investment goals. Core strategies focus on stable income-producing properties, value-add strategies involve adding value through improvements, and opportunistic strategies target high-risk, high-reward investments.

Distressed investing involves acquiring financially troubled properties, and specialized sector investments concentrate on specific asset types. By understanding the different types of private equity real estate investments, investors can tailor their portfolios to align with their risk tolerance and investment objectives.

1.3 The Private Equity Real Estate Investment Lifecycle

In this section, we will cover the essential aspects of private equity real estate investing lifecycle. We'll explore fund formation, deal sourcing, due diligence, asset management, and exit strategies. These key points encompass raising capital, identifying investment opportunities, evaluating properties, implementing value creation strategies, and maximizing returns through various exit approaches. Understanding these elements is crucial for successful private equity real estate investing.

The private equity real estate investment lifecycle can be broken down into five key stages: *fund formation*, *deal sourcing*, *due diligence*, *asset management*, and *exit strategies*. Understanding these stages can help investors gain insights into the private equity real estate investment process and the factors that drive returns.

1. The first stage of the private equity real estate investment lifecycle is **fund formation**. This stage involves raising capital from investors to invest in real estate assets. Private equity real estate funds typically have a *fixed life span* and require a *significant amount of capital* to achieve diversification and scale. Fund managers must have a track record of success and a compelling investment strategy to attract investors. The fund formation stage also involves setting up the legal and governance framework for the fund.
2. The second stage is **deal sourcing**, where the fund manager

identifies and evaluates potential real estate investment opportunities. Deal sourcing involves developing relationships with brokers, property owners, and other market participants to access a broad range of investment opportunities. Fund managers may also leverage their industry expertise and market insights to *identify off-market opportunities* and gain a competitive advantage. Deal evaluation involves assessing factors such as property condition, location, tenant quality, and market trends to determine whether the investment meets the fund's investment criteria.

3. The third stage is **due diligence**, which involves conducting a *comprehensive analysis* of the investment opportunity. Due diligence encompasses *property viability analysis, market analysis, financial evaluation*, and *legal and tax assessment*. This stage involves gathering information from various sources, including property inspections, market data, financial statements, and legal documentation. Due diligence is critical to identifying and mitigating potential risks associated with the investment.

4. The fourth stage is **asset management**, where the fund manager actively manages the real estate assets to generate value. Asset management involves developing and implementing value creation strategies such as *property upgrades, lease negotiations, tenant management*, and *operational improvements*. Fund managers must have the expertise and resources to effectively manage the assets, mitigate risks, and optimize returns. Effective asset management requires close collaboration with property managers, leasing agents, and other service providers.

5. The final stage is **exit strategies**, where the fund manager maximizes returns through *sales, recapitalizations*, or

refinancing. Exit strategies involve *assessing market conditions, evaluating the property's performance,* and *determining the best approach* to exit the investment. The goal of exit strategies is to realize the investment's potential value, distribute the proceeds to investors, and achieve the fund's investment objectives. Exit strategies are a critical aspect of the private equity real estate investment process and require careful planning and execution.

In conclusion, the private equity real estate investment lifecycle involves five key stages: fund formation, deal sourcing, due diligence, asset management, and exit strategies. Each stage requires specialized expertise and resources to achieve successful outcomes. By understanding the private equity real estate investment process, investors can gain insights into the factors that drive returns and make informed investment decisions.

1.4 Key Players in Private Equity Real Estate

Understanding the roles and contributions of these key players is essential for navigating the world of private equity real estate. In this section, we will explore the key players involved in private equity real estate. This includes the structure, strategies, and investment focus of private equity real estate firms. We will also discuss the roles of limited partners (LPs) as investors in private equity real estate funds, general partners (GPs) as fund managers, real estate operators responsible for property management, and various service providers offering legal, financial, and advisory support for real estate investments.

Private equity real estate firms are the entities that manage and operate private equity real estate funds. These firms are responsible for the *overall investment strategy, fund management,* and *execution of real estate investments.* They often have a *team of professionals* with expertise in real estate acquisitions, asset management, and investment analysis. Private equity real estate firms have a structured approach to investing, which includes defining the investment focus, targeting specific asset classes or regions, and implementing various investment strategies.

Limited partners (LPs) are the investors who *provide capital* to private equity real estate funds. LPs can be institutional investors, such as *pension funds, endowments,* and *insurance companies,* as well as *high-net-worth individuals.* LPs invest in private equity real estate funds with the expectation of generating attractive risk-adjusted returns and diversifying their investment portfolios. They commit capital to the fund and become passive investors, relying on the expertise and track record of the general partners.

General partners (GPs) are *the managers* of private equity real estate funds. GPs are responsible for the *day-to-day operations* of the fund, including *deal sourcing, due diligence, asset management,* and *investor relations.* They play a crucial role in identifying and executing investment opportunities, managing the fund's portfolio, and delivering returns to the LPs. GPs typically earn *management fees* and *carried interest,* which is a share of the profits generated by the fund.

Real estate operators are experts in *property management* and *operations.* They are responsible for the *day-to-day management* and *maintenance* of the real estate assets within the fund's portfolio. Real estate operators ensure that properties are *well-maintained, leases are managed,* and *tenant relationships are nurtured.* They may handle property-level financials, tenant negotiations, lease renewals, and other operational aspects. Real estate operators work closely with the fund managers to execute the asset management strategies and enhance the value of the properties.

Service providers play a crucial role in supporting private equity real estate investments. These providers include *legal firms, financial* *institutions*, and *advisory firms* that offer specialized services to facilitate real estate transactions.

1. **Legal providers** assist in structuring investment vehicles, drafting legal agreements, and ensuring compliance with regulatory requirements.
2. **Financial institutions** provide financing solutions, such as debt or equity capital, to support the acquisition and development of real estate assets.
3. **Advisory firms** offer strategic guidance, market analysis, and due diligence support to help investors make informed investment decisions.

In summary, key players in private equity real estate include private equity real estate firms, limited partners (LPs), general partners (GPs), real estate operators, and service providers. Each player has a distinct role and contributes to the successful execution and operation of private equity real estate investments. Their collective expertise and collaboration help drive returns, manage risks, and create value in the dynamic real estate market.

1.5 Benefits and Considerations of Private Equity Real Estate Investing

Private equity real estate investing offers a range of benefits and considerations that investors should carefully evaluate. These include the potential for *strong returns* and *portfolio diversification, access to professional expertise and market knowledge, mitigating risks* through active management and value creation, *liquidity considerations and lock-up periods,* as well as *regulatory and market factors* impacting private equity real estate.

One significant benefit of private equity real estate investing is the **potential for strong returns and portfolio diversification**. Real estate investments have historically delivered competitive risk-adjusted returns, offering the potential for capital appreciation and income generation. Private equity real estate investments, in particular, often target value-add or opportunistic strategies, which aim to create value through active management and property improvements. These strategies have the potential to generate higher returns compared to traditional, publicly traded real estate investments. Additionally, real estate has historically exhibited low correlation with other financial assets, making it an effective diversification tool that can help reduce overall portfolio risk.

Investing in private equity real estate also provides **access to professional expertise and market knowledge**. Private equity real estate firms have specialized teams with extensive experience in property acquisitions, asset management, and investment analysis. They have the *market knowledge* and resources to *identify attractive investment opportunities* and *navigate complex real estate transactions*. By investing in private equity real estate funds, investors can leverage the expertise of these professionals and benefit from their ability to identify value-add opportunities and execute effective investment strategies.

Mitigating risks is another consideration in private equity real estate investing. Active management and value creation strategies implemented by private equity real estate firms can help mitigate risks associated with real estate investments. Through hands-on management, these firms can *enhance property performance, optimize cash flows,* and *mitigate potential downside risks.* Value-add strategies, such as property renovations or repositioning, can also lead to increased property value and enhanced returns. The ability to actively manage and add value to real estate assets sets private equity real estate investments apart from passive, publicly traded real estate investments.

Liquidity considerations and **lock-up periods** are important factors to consider in private equity real estate investing. Private equity real estate funds typically have a fixed term, and investors' capital is locked up for the duration of the fund's life, which can range from several years to a decade or more. This illiquid nature of private equity real estate investments means that *investors may not have immediate access to their capital* during the investment period. Investors should carefully evaluate their liquidity needs and investment time horizon before committing to private equity real estate investments.

Lastly, private equity real estate investing is subject to **regulatory and market factors** that can impact investment returns. Regulatory changes, such as *tax policies*, *zoning regulations*, or *environmental regulations*, can affect the profitability and feasibility of real estate investments. Additionally, market conditions, such as *interest rates*, *economic cycles*, or *supply and demand dynamics*, can impact property values and rental income. It is essential for investors to stay informed about these factors and assess how they may influence their private equity real estate investments.

In summary, private equity real estate investing offers potential benefits such as strong returns, portfolio diversification, access to professional expertise, and risk mitigation through active management. However, investors should also consider factors like liquidity considerations, lock-up periods, and regulatory and market factors that can impact their investments. By carefully evaluating these benefits and considerations, investors can make informed decisions and determine whether private equity real estate investing aligns with their investment goals and risk tolerance.

Conclusion

In conclusion, private equity real estate investing offers opportunities for investors to generate profits through real estate assets. It is essential to carefully consider the advantages and risks associated with this investment strategy, and to engage with knowledgeable professionals to make informed decisions and effectively manage investments.

Chapter 2: How to Set Up a Private Equity Real Estate Investing Firm

Business - Photo by RDNE Stock project

2.1 Defining Your Investment Strategy and Business Plan

When embarking on a private equity real estate investment journey, it is crucial to define your investment strategy and develop a comprehensive business plan. This involves identifying your target market and investment focus, establishing investment criteria and risk appetite, conducting market research and analysis, and setting realistic financial goals and performance targets.

1. To start, you need to **identify your target market** and **investment focus**. This includes determining the *types of properties* you are interested in investing in and the *geographic regions* you want to focus on. Property types can vary widely, including residential, commercial, industrial, hospitality, or healthcare properties. Geographic regions can range from local to national or even international markets. By narrowing

down your target market and investment focus, you can focus your efforts and resources more effectively.

2. Once you have identified your target market and investment focus, it is important to **establish your investment criteria and risk appetite**. This involves defining the specific characteristics and parameters you are looking for in potential investment opportunities. For example, you may have preferences regarding *property size*, *location*, *condition*, or *cash flow potential*. Additionally, you need to determine your risk appetite by assessing the *level of risk* you are willing to take on in your investments. This can be influenced by factors such as your investment horizon, available capital, and overall investment strategy.

3. **Conducting thorough market research and analysis** is another crucial step in defining your investment strategy. This involves studying *market trends*, *supply and demand dynamics*, *economic indicators*, and *demographic factors* that can impact the performance of real estate investments. Market research can help you identify emerging opportunities, understand market cycles, and make informed investment decisions. By analyzing market data and trends, you can gain insights into potential risks and opportunities in your target market.

4. **Developing a comprehensive business plan** is essential to guide your investment strategy and decision-making process. A business plan outlines your *investment goals*, *strategies*, and *operational plans*. It should include details about your target market, investment criteria, acquisition strategies, asset management plans, and exit strategies. A well-defined business plan serves as a roadmap for your investments and provides a clear framework for evaluating potential opportunities.

5. Lastly, **setting realistic financial goals** and **performance**

targets is critical. This involves determining your *return expectations, cash flow requirements,* and *investment timelines.* It is important to establish achievable goals that align with your risk appetite and investment strategy. Realistic financial goals provide a benchmark for evaluating the success of your investments and help guide your decision-making process.

In summary, defining your investment strategy and developing a comprehensive business plan are crucial steps in private equity real estate investing. This involves identifying your target market and investment focus, establishing investment criteria and risk appetite, conducting market research and analysis, and setting realistic financial goals and performance targets. By carefully defining your strategy and planning your investments, you can enhance your chances of success and achieve your investment objectives in the dynamic world of private equity real estate.

2.2 Structuring Your Firm and Legal Considerations

When structuring your private equity real estate firm, there are several important legal considerations to take into account. These include choosing the appropriate legal entity, working with legal counsel to draft operating agreements and partnership agreements, understanding regulatory requirements and compliance obligations, establishing governance and decision-making processes, and addressing taxation and accounting considerations.

1. Choosing the **appropriate legal entity** is a crucial decision that will impact the structure and operations of your firm. Common options for private equity real estate firms include *limited liability companies (LLCs)* and *limited partnerships (LPs).* LLCs provide flexibility in terms of management and ownership, while LPs offer a clear distinction between

general partners (GPs) and limited partners (LPs) in terms of liability and decision-making authority. Selecting the most suitable legal entity will depend on factors such as the size of your firm, the number of partners involved, and your specific business goals.

2. Working with legal counsel is essential when **drafting operating agreements and partnership agreements**. These agreements outline the rights, responsibilities, and obligations of the partners involved in the firm. They address key areas such as capital contributions, profit and loss allocation, decision-making processes, and procedures for admitting or withdrawing partners. Legal counsel will ensure that these agreements are properly drafted to protect the interests of all parties involved and provide a clear framework for the operation of the firm.

3. **Understanding regulatory requirements and compliance obligations** is crucial to ensure your firm operates within the legal framework. Private equity real estate firms may be subject to various regulations, such as *securities laws* and *anti-money laundering* regulations. It is important to be aware of these requirements and establish procedures and internal controls to ensure *compliance*. This may involve conducting thorough due diligence on investors, implementing *know-your-customer (KYC)* procedures, and adhering to reporting and disclosure obligations.

4. **Establishing governance and decision-making processes** is essential for the smooth operation of your firm. This includes defining the *roles and responsibilities of partners*, establishing *voting rights and decision-making procedures*, and implementing a *clear system of governance*. Having well-defined governance structures ensures transparency, accountability, and effective decision-making within the firm.

5. **Taxation and accounting considerations** are also important factors to address when structuring your private equity real estate firm. This involves working with *tax professionals* and *accountants* to understand the tax implications of different legal entities and investment strategies. They can provide guidance on tax-efficient structuring, compliance with tax regulations, and proper accounting practices.

In summary, structuring your private equity real estate firm involves important legal considerations. This includes choosing the appropriate legal entity, working with legal counsel to draft operating and partnership agreements, understanding regulatory requirements and compliance obligations, establishing governance and decision-making processes, and addressing taxation and accounting considerations. By addressing these legal considerations, you can ensure that your firm operates within the legal framework, protects the interests of all parties involved, and sets a solid foundation for success in the private equity real estate industry.

2.3 Fundraising and Investor Relations

Fundraising and investor relations are critical aspects of private equity real estate. This section focuses on creating a compelling pitch deck and marketing materials, identifying and approaching potential investors, conducting investor due diligence and qualification, structuring your fund and capitalization plan, and negotiating terms and conditions with limited partners.

1. To successfully raise capital for your private equity real estate fund, you need to **create a compelling pitch deck and marketing materials.** These materials should effectively communicate your investment strategy, track record, and value proposition to potential investors. The pitch deck

should provide a clear overview of your *firm, investment approach, target market, competitive advantage*, and *projected returns*. It should be visually appealing, concise, and persuasive, highlighting the unique aspects that differentiate your fund from others in the market.

2. **Identifying and approaching potential investors** is the next step in the fundraising process. This involves conducting market research and building a *targeted list of potential investors* who align with your investment strategy and risk appetite. These investors can include *high-net-worth individuals, family offices, institutional investors*, and *pension funds*. Once you have identified your target investors, you can develop a tailored approach to engage with them. This may include attending industry conferences, networking events, or utilizing personal connections to establish relationships with potential investors.

3. **Conducting investor due diligence and qualification** is crucial to ensure that the investors align with your fund's objectives and requirements. This process involves gathering information about potential investors' *investment preferences, risk tolerance, investment size*, and *track record*. It is essential to *screen potential investors* to ensure they meet your fund's minimum investment requirements and share your long-term vision. Additionally, performing *background checks* and verifying the legitimacy and reputation of potential investors is an important step in mitigating risks.

4. **Structuring your fund and capitalization plan** is a critical aspect of the fundraising process. This involves determining the *fund's structure*, including the target *fund size, management fee structure*, and *carried interest allocation*. The *capitalization plan* outlines how the fund will raise and deploy capital over its lifespan. This plan may include

multiple closings, capital commitments from limited partners, and capital calls to meet investment needs. It is important to establish a clear and transparent structure that aligns the interests of the fund manager and the limited partners.

5. **Negotiating terms and conditions** with limited partners is the final step in the fundraising process. This involves discussing and finalizing the legal and financial aspects of the partnership. Key considerations in these negotiations include the *management fee, carried interest, distribution waterfall, governance rights, reporting obligations*, and *exit strategies*. The negotiation process requires careful consideration of both parties' interests to reach mutually beneficial agreements.

In summary, fundraising and investor relations are crucial for the success of private equity real estate funds. This involves creating a compelling pitch deck and marketing materials, identifying and approaching potential investors, conducting investor due diligence and qualification, structuring the fund and capitalization plan, and negotiating terms and conditions with limited partners. By effectively executing these steps, you can attract the right investors, build strong relationships, and raise the necessary capital to execute your investment strategy in the private equity real estate market.

2.4 Fund Operations and Infrastructure

Fund operations and infrastructure are essential for the effective management and growth of a private equity real estate fund. This section focuses on *building a strong team, establishing office space and technology systems, implementing risk management and compliance frameworks, setting up reporting systems*, and *building relationships with service providers*.

1. **Building a strong team** is crucial for the success of a private equity real estate fund. This involves hiring key roles such as *investment professionals, fund administrators,* and *operations staff. Investment professionals* play a critical role in sourcing and evaluating investment opportunities, executing transactions, and managing the fund's portfolio. *Fund administrators* provide administrative support, including fund accounting, investor reporting, and regulatory compliance. It is important to hire individuals with relevant expertise, experience, and a strong track record in the private equity real estate industry.
2. **Establishing office space, technology systems, and operational infrastructure** is vital for the smooth operation of the fund.
   1. This includes *securing office space* that accommodates the needs of the team and provides a professional environment for conducting business.
   2. *Technology systems* should be implemented to support efficient operations, data management, and communication within the firm. This may include investment management software, customer relationship management (CRM) systems, and secure data storage solutions.
   3. Additionally, *operational infrastructure* such as back-office processes, documentation management, and compliance systems should be established to ensure proper governance and operational efficiency.
3. **Implementing robust risk management and compliance frameworks** is essential for managing risks and ensuring regulatory compliance. Private equity real estate funds are exposed to various risks, including market risk, operational risk, and legal and regulatory risk. A comprehensive risk

management framework should be established to identify, assess, and mitigate these risks. This includes implementing *risk assessment processes*, *monitoring key risk indicators*, and *developing contingency plans*. Compliance frameworks should also be established to ensure *adherence to applicable laws and regulations*, including anti-money laundering (AML) and know-your-customer (KYC) requirements.

4. **Setting up reporting systems** for investors and regulatory authorities is necessary to provide *transparency* and fulfill *reporting obligations*. Private equity real estate funds are required to provide regular reports to investors, including *financial statements*, *performance updates*, and *investment summaries*. Additionally, regulatory authorities may require specific reporting on areas such as *investor disclosures*, *investment activities*, and *compliance matters*. Establishing robust reporting systems and processes ensures accurate and timely reporting to investors and regulatory bodies.

5. **Building relationships with service providers** is essential for obtaining specialized expertise and support. Private equity real estate funds often require the services of external providers, such as *legal counsel*, *accounting firms*, *custodians*, and *valuation firms*. These service providers play a critical role in providing legal, financial, and advisory support to the fund. Building strong relationships with these service providers ensures access to their expertise, enhances operational efficiency, and enables the fund to meet its legal, financial, and regulatory requirements.

In summary, fund operations and infrastructure are critical components of managing a private equity real estate fund. Building a strong team, establishing office space and technology systems, implementing risk management and compliance frameworks, setting up reporting systems, and building relationships with service providers are essential for the effective and efficient management of the fund. By establishing robust operational infrastructure and implementing best practices, private equity real estate funds can enhance their ability to execute their investment strategy, meet regulatory obligations, and deliver value to their investors.

2.5 Deal Sourcing and Execution

Deal sourcing and execution are critical aspects of private equity real estate investing. This section focuses on *developing a network for deal sourcing, conducting rigorous due diligence, evaluating property valuations and financial projections, negotiating purchase and sale agreements,* and *implementing a structured approach to asset management and value creation.*

1. **Developing a network for deal sourcing** is essential to identify potential investment opportunities. This network can include *brokers, real estate agents, industry contacts,* and *other professionals* in the real estate industry. Building strong relationships and staying connected with these individuals and organizations can provide access to off-market deals, market insights, and potential partnerships. Actively engaging with the network and maintaining a reputation as a reliable and credible investor can enhance deal flow and increase the chances of finding attractive investment opportunities.

2. **Conducting rigorous due diligence** is a crucial step in the investment process. This involves performing a *comprehensive analysis of potential investments* to evaluate their viability, risks, and potential returns. Due diligence typically includes reviewing *property documentation, financial statements, lease agreements,* and *market data.* It may also involve conducting

site visits, *environmental assessments*, and *legal reviews*. Thorough due diligence helps identify potential issues or risks associated with the investment and enables informed investment decisions.

3. **Evaluating property valuations, financial projections, and market dynamics** is an important aspect of deal execution.
    1. This includes analyzing the *property's value* based on various factors such as *location, condition, income potential*, and *market comparables*.
    2. *Financial projections* should be carefully reviewed to assess the property's *income potential, cash flow*, and *potential for appreciation*.
    3. Understanding *market dynamics*, including *supply and demand factors, vacancy rates*, and *rental trends*, is crucial in assessing the property's potential for long-term success. These evaluations provide a foundation for determining the investment's potential returns and risks.

4. **Negotiating purchase and sale agreements, financing, and legal documentation** is a critical step in finalizing the deal. This involves engaging in negotiations with sellers, lenders, and legal counsel to establish the terms and conditions of the transaction.
    1. *Purchase and sale agreements* outline the terms of the transaction, including purchase price, closing conditions, and representations and warranties.
    2. *Financing arrangements*, if applicable, are negotiated with lenders to secure the necessary funds for the acquisition.
    3. Legal documentation, such as closing documents and title transfers, must be prepared and reviewed to ensure a smooth and legally compliant transaction.

5. Implementing a **structured approach to asset management and value creation** is essential for maximizing the investment's potential.

    1. This includes developing a *detailed asset management plan* that outlines strategies for operational improvements, renovation or redevelopment initiatives, tenant retention, and lease optimization.

    2. *Active management of the property*, including regular monitoring of performance, expenses, and market conditions, helps identify opportunities for value creation and ensures that the investment aligns with the fund's objectives.

    3. *Regular reporting* to investors and stakeholders keeps them informed about the progress and performance of the investment.

In summary, deal sourcing and execution are crucial steps in private equity real estate investing. Developing a network for deal sourcing, conducting rigorous due diligence, evaluating property valuations and financial projections, negotiating purchase and sale agreements, and implementing a structured approach to asset management and value creation are key components of successful deal execution. By leveraging networks, conducting thorough due diligence, evaluating investment opportunities, and implementing effective asset management strategies, private equity real estate investors can increase the likelihood of achieving their investment objectives and delivering value to their stakeholders.

Conclusion

In conclusion, setting up a private equity real estate investing firm involves several key steps and considerations. Strategic planning helps define the firm's target market, investment focus, and financial goals, enabling it to allocate resources effectively and pursue opportunities that align with its objectives. Legal compliance is essential in choosing the appropriate legal entity, drafting agreements, and adhering to regulatory requirements to ensure the firm operates within the legal framework. By carefully considering these aspects, a private equity real estate investing firm can establish a strong foundation for success and navigate the complexities of the industry with confidence.

Chapter 3: Financing Private Equity Real Estate Investments

Real Estate Financing - Photo by nattanan23

3.1 Introduction to Private Equity Real Estate Financing

Private equity real estate financing plays a crucial role in the success of investment objectives. This section provides an introduction to private equity real estate financing, emphasizing the importance of proper financing, understanding different financing options, balancing debt and equity strategies, and the role of risk management in financing decisions.

1. **Proper financing** is essential to achieving investment objectives in private equity real estate. Whether it's acquiring properties, funding development projects, or optimizing existing assets, access to appropriate financing enables investors to execute their strategies effectively. Financing provides the necessary capital to *acquire properties, cover*

operational expenses, and *implement value-add initiatives*. It also allows investors to leverage their investments, potentially amplifying returns. Proper financing ensures that the investment is *adequately capitalized* and aligns with the specific goals and risk tolerance of the investment strategy.

2. There are different types of **financing options** available in private equity real estate. *Debt financing* involves borrowing money from lenders, such as banks or financial institutions, and repaying the principal amount plus interest over a specified period. *Equity financing*, on the other hand, involves raising capital from investors who become partial owners of the property or the fund. It is important to understand the advantages and disadvantages of each financing option. Debt financing offers the benefit of *leverage* and *potential tax advantages*, but it also involves *interest payments* and *debt service* obligations. Equity financing provides *more flexibility* and may be *less risky*, but it *dilutes ownership* and *reduces potential returns*.

3. **Balancing debt and equity financing strategies** is crucial in private equity real estate. The optimal mix of debt and equity depends on factors such as the *investment strategy*, *risk profile*, and *market conditions*. High leverage through debt financing can *amplify returns* in a rising market but may also increase the risk of financial distress in a downturn. Equity financing provides *more stability* but can limit the potential for higher returns. Striking the right balance between debt and equity financing is essential to manage risk, optimize returns, and align with the investment objectives and risk appetite of the fund.

4. **Risk management** plays a vital role in making financing decisions. Private equity real estate investments are exposed to various risks, including market risk, operational risk, and

financing risk. Assessing and managing these risks are critical to ensuring the long-term viability and success of the investment. Proper risk management involves evaluating the *financial strength* of the investment, analyzing *market conditions*, assessing the stability of *rental income*, and stress-testing the investment under different scenarios.

In summary, private equity real estate financing is essential to achieving investment objectives. Proper financing allows investors to acquire properties, fund development projects, and optimize assets. Understanding the different financing options, balancing debt and equity strategies, and considering risk management in financing decisions are important aspects of the process. By carefully evaluating financing options, striking the right balance between debt and equity, and managing risks effectively, private equity real estate investors can maximize their chances of success and achieve their investment objectives.

3.2 Debt Financing

Debt financing is a common form of financing in private equity real estate that involves borrowing money from lenders to fund property acquisitions or development projects. This section provides an overview of the types of debt financing available, the pros and cons of debt financing, the structuring of debt financing deals, factors that impact loan terms and interest rates, and the sources of debt financing.

There are various types of debt financing available in private equity real estate.

1. **Commercial mortgages** are one of the most common forms of debt financing, where lenders provide loans secured by the property being acquired or developed.

2. **Mezzanine financing** is another type of debt financing that combines elements of debt and equity. Mezzanine lenders provide capital that sits in a subordinated position to the senior debt, often taking the form of a loan or preferred equity.
3. **Bridge loans** are short-term loans that help bridge the gap between the acquisition or development of a property and the long-term financing. These loans are typically used when there is a time-sensitive opportunity or when the property requires renovation or repositioning before it qualifies for permanent financing.

Debt financing offers several advantages and disadvantages.

1. The main advantage is that it allows investors to **leverage their investments** and potentially achieve higher returns.
2. Debt financing also provides **access to capital** that may not be readily available through equity financing.
3. Additionally, interest payments on debt financing may be **tax-deductible**, providing potential tax advantages.

However, debt financing also carries certain risks.

1. The main disadvantage is the **obligation to repay** the principal amount plus interest, which increases the financial burden on the investment.
2. High levels of debt can increase the **risk of default**, especially in an economic downturn.

Structuring debt financing deals involves negotiating the terms and conditions of the loan. This includes determining the loan amount, *interest rate, repayment period*, and any *associated fees* or covenants. The loan structure may also involve establishing *collateral* and determining the *priority of repayment* in the event of default. Negotiating favorable terms is crucial to ensure that the debt financing aligns with the investment objectives and risk profile of the project.

Several factors impact loan terms and interest rates in debt financing. These include the *creditworthiness* of the borrower, the *loan-to-value ratio*, the property's *cash flow* and performance projections, the *market conditions*, and the prevailing *interest rates in the market*. Lenders assess these factors to determine the risk level of the loan and set appropriate terms and interest rates. Borrowers with stronger credit profiles, lower loan-to-value ratios, and favorable property performance projections are likely to secure more favorable loan terms and lower interest rates.

There are various sources of debt financing available in private equity real estate. These include *commercial banks, insurance companies, pension funds, private debt funds*, and *alternative lenders*.

1. **Commercial banks** are traditional lenders that offer a range of financing options, including commercial mortgages. Insurance companies and pension funds often provide long-term financing for stabilized properties.
2. **Private debt funds** specialize in providing debt financing to real estate projects and may offer more flexible terms.
3. Alternative lenders, such as **crowdfunding platforms** or **online marketplace lenders**, have emerged as additional sources of debt financing, providing alternative options for borrowers.

In summary, debt financing is an important aspect of private equity real estate investing. It provides access to capital, allows for leverage, and potentially enhances returns. Different types of debt financing, including commercial mortgages, mezzanine financing, and bridge loans, offer flexibility depending on the investment objectives. While debt financing carries risks and requires repayment obligations, it can be structured to align with the project's risk profile and cash flow projections. Understanding the factors that impact loan terms and interest rates and exploring various sources of debt financing enables investors to secure the most suitable financing options for their private equity real estate projects.

3.3 Equity Financing

Equity financing is another common form of financing in private equity real estate that involves raising capital from investors who become partial owners of the property or the fund. This section provides an overview of the types of equity financing available, the pros and cons of equity financing, the structuring of equity financing deals, understanding investment structures and risk profiles, and the sources of equity financing.

There are various types of equity financing available in private equity real estate.

1. **Joint ventures (JVs)** are a common form of equity financing where *two or more parties pool their resources and expertise* to invest in a real estate project. Each party contributes capital and shares the risks and rewards of the investment.
2. **Preferred equity** is another type of equity financing where *investors provide capital in exchange for preferred rights* and a priority position in terms of distributions and repayment.
3. **Common equity** is the most basic form of equity financing where *investors become shareholders* and have ownership rights proportional to their investment.

Equity financing offers several advantages and disadvantages.

1. One of the main advantages is that it **provides more**

flexibility in terms of capital and structure. Equity financing can be structured to align with the investment objectives, risk profile, and cash flow projections of the project.

2. It also allows investors to **participate in the potential upside** of the investment.

3. Additionally, unlike debt financing, equity financing **does not involve regular interest payments** or strict repayment obligations.

4. However, equity financing may **dilute ownership** and **reduce the potential returns** for the initial investors.

5. It also requires **sharing control** and decision-making with other equity investors.

Structuring equity financing deals involves negotiating the **terms and conditions** of the investment. This includes determining the equity *ownership percentage*, *distribution rights*, *governance structure*, and *exit strategies*.

The structure of the equity financing deal depends on factors such as the *investment strategy*, the *risk profile of the project*, and the *preferences of the investors*. It is important to carefully consider these factors and strike a balance that aligns the interests of the investors and ensures a mutually beneficial partnership.

Understanding investment structures and risk profiles is crucial in equity financing. Different investment structures, such as funds, syndications, or single asset investments, have different risk profiles and return expectations.

1. **Funds** typically invest in a diversified portfolio of properties, spreading the risk across multiple assets.

2. **Syndications** involve a group of investors pooling their resources for a specific property investment.

3. **Single asset investments** focus on individual properties and carry a higher concentration of risk.

There are various sources of equity financing available in private equity real estate. These include *institutional investors* such as pension funds, insurance companies, and endowments, as well as *high-net-worth individuals*, *family offices*, and *private equity firms*.

1. **Institutional investors** often allocate a portion of their investment portfolio to real estate and seek opportunities to invest in private equity real estate funds or joint ventures.
2. **High-net-worth individuals** and **family offices** may invest directly in specific real estate projects or participate in syndications.
3. **Private equity firms** may provide equity financing through their investment funds or partner with other investors on joint ventures.

In summary, equity financing is an important component of private equity real estate investing. It offers flexibility, potential for higher returns, and alignment of interests between investors and the project. Different types of equity financing, provide varying structures and rights for investors. Understanding the advantages and disadvantages, structuring the deals appropriately, and considering the risk profiles associated with different investment structures help investors navigate the equity financing landscape.

3.4 Tax Considerations in Private Equity Real Estate Financing

Tax considerations play a significant role in private equity real estate financing, as they can impact the overall profitability of the investment. This section provides an overview of the tax implications of different financing structures, understanding tax benefits and liabilities, tax planning strategies for financing deals, minimizing tax exposure, and the importance of working with tax professionals to optimize financing structures.

The choice of financing structure in private equity real estate can have tax implications for both the investors and the investment vehicle.

1. **Debt financing** offers the advantage of *deducting interest expenses*, which can reduce taxable income and lower the tax liability.
2. **Equity financing,** on the other hand, may provide *long-term capital gains treatment* for investors, which could result in lower tax rates. However, equity financing may also involve *additional tax compliance* requirements, such as partnership tax filings or distribution reporting.

Tax planning strategies play a vital role in structuring financing deals to optimize tax benefits and minimize tax exposure. For example, allocating deductible expenses to the highest-tax bracket investors or utilizing tax-efficient investment vehicles can help maximize after-tax returns. It is important to consider the tax implications at the entity level, as well as for individual investors, to ensure tax-efficient structures and minimize any potential tax risks.

Minimizing tax exposure and maximizing returns in private equity real estate financing requires a comprehensive tax strategy. This includes considering the timing of income recognition, utilizing tax credits and deductions, and structuring investments in tax-favorable jurisdictions. Additionally, investors may explore tax-deferred exchanges, such as like-kind exchanges under Section 1031 of the Internal Revenue Code, to defer capital gains taxes when disposing of properties and reinvesting in new ones.

Working with tax professionals who specialize in real estate taxation is crucial to optimizing financing structures and maximizing tax benefits. These professionals can provide valuable guidance on *structuring transactions, identifying tax planning opportunities,* and *ensuring compliance* with applicable tax laws and regulations. By leveraging their expertise, investors can navigate the complex tax landscape, make informed decisions, and achieve tax-efficient financing structures that align with their investment objectives.

In summary, tax considerations are an essential aspect of private equity real estate financing. The choice of financing structure can have significant tax implications for both investors and investment vehicles. Understanding the tax benefits and liabilities associated with different financing structures, implementing tax planning strategies, and working with tax professionals are crucial steps to minimize tax exposure and maximize after-tax returns. By carefully considering tax implications and optimizing financing structures, investors can enhance the overall profitability of their private equity real estate investments.

3.5 Evaluating Financing Options for Private Equity Real Estate Investments

When it comes to private equity real estate investments, evaluating financing options is a crucial step in the decision-making process. This section focuses on the key considerations involved in evaluating financing options, including conducting a comprehensive financial analysis, evaluating risk and return profiles, assessing liquidity and exit strategies, developing a structured approach to financing decisions, and aligning financing strategies with investment objectives.

Conducting a comprehensive financial analysis is essential to assess the feasibility and profitability of potential deals. This analysis includes evaluating the *projected cash flows,* assessing the impact of financing costs on the *overall returns*, and analyzing the expected *return on investment (ROI)* and *internal rate of return (IRR)*. By carefully examining the financial aspects of the investment, investors can gain insights into the potential risks and rewards associated with different financing options.

Evaluating the risk and return profiles of different financing options is critical in determining the most suitable approach. *Debt financing typically offers lower risk* as it involves regular interest payments and a defined repayment schedule. On the other hand, *equity financing carries higher risk* but also potential for higher returns, as investors participate in the upside of the investment. By assessing the risk and return trade-offs, investors can make informed decisions regarding the mix of debt and equity financing that aligns with their risk appetite and investment objectives.

Assessing liquidity and exit strategies is another important factor when evaluating financing options. Private equity real estate investments often involve longer investment horizons, and *liquidity can be limited* compared to other asset classes. It is crucial to assess the availability of exit strategies such as *selling the property*, *refinancing*, or *recapitalizing* to ensure that the chosen financing option supports the desired exit timeline and aligns with the overall investment strategy.

Developing a structured approach to financing decisions involves considering factors such as the *cost of capital*, *financing terms*, *covenants*, and *potential risks* associated with each financing option. This requires evaluating multiple scenarios, stress testing the financial projections, and assessing the impact of market conditions and interest rate fluctuations on the investment. By taking a systematic and analytical approach to financing decisions, investors can make informed choices that maximize returns and mitigate risks.

Aligning financing strategies with investment objectives is crucial for successful private equity real estate investments. The financing approach should support the overall *investment strategy*, *risk tolerance*, and *long-term objectives*. For example, if the investment objective is to generate stable income, debt financing may be more suitable. Conversely, if the objective is capital appreciation, a higher proportion of equity financing may be considered. By aligning the financing strategy with the investment objectives, investors can ensure that the chosen financing options contribute to the overall success of the investment.

In summary, evaluating financing options in private equity real estate requires a comprehensive analysis of the financial aspects, risk and return profiles, liquidity considerations, and alignment with investment objectives. By conducting a thorough financial analysis, assessing risk and return trade-offs, evaluating liquidity and exit strategies, and aligning financing decisions with investment objectives, investors can make informed choices that support the overall success of their private equity real estate investments.

Conclusion

Private equity real estate financing is crucial for achieving investment goals. This section covered key concepts and terminologies related to financing options in private equity real estate, including debt and equity financing. It discussed the pros and cons of each option, factors influencing loan terms, and various types of equity financing. The importance of tax considerations and conducting a comprehensive financial analysis, risk assessment, and aligning financing strategies with investment objectives were highlighted. Proper financing enables investors to leverage capital, acquire properties, and optimize cash flows while mitigating risks. By understanding these concepts and implementing effective financing strategies, investors can increase their chances of success in the private equity real estate market.

49

Chapter 4: What is the Private Equity Capital Stack?

Capital Stack - Photo by 8385

4.1 Introduction to the Capital Stack in Private Equity

The capital stack is a fundamental concept in private equity and real estate investing. This section provides an introduction to the capital stack, highlights its importance in private equity, explores the hierarchy of capital sources, discusses the role of the capital stack in risk assessment and investment structuring, and introduces key terminologies associated with the capital stack.

The capital stack refers to the different **layers or components of capital** invested in a real estate project or private equity investment. It represents the combination of debt and equity financing that contributes to the total capital structure of the investment. The capital stack is typically depicted as a vertical representation, with each layer representing a different type of capital source.

The capital stack is organized in a hierarchical structure, with each layer having a specific position in terms of **repayment priority**. The hierarchy typically starts with *senior debt*, followed by *mezzanine debt*, *preferred equity*, and *common equity*.

1. **Senior debt** holders have the highest priority in repayment and are typically secured by the underlying assets.
2. **Mezzanine debt** and **preferred equity** holders fall in the middle of the capital stack and have a lower priority than senior debt but higher priority than common equity.
3. **Common equity** holders have the highest risk and potential for returns but also the lowest priority in terms of repayment.

By analyzing the capital stack, investors can assess the **risk exposure** at each layer and make informed decisions regarding the allocation of capital.

The capital stack also influences the **investment structure**, as it determines the cost of capital, the potential returns for each layer, and the overall risk profile of the investment.

In summary, the capital stack is a vital concept in private equity and real estate investing. Understanding the capital stack is crucial for assessing risk, structuring investments, and making informed decisions. By examining the hierarchy of capital sources, evaluating the risk exposure at each layer, and considering key terminologies related to the capital stack, investors can effectively analyze investment opportunities, allocate capital strategically, and maximize their chances of success in private equity and real estate ventures.

4.2 Components of the Private Equity Capital Stack

The private equity capital stack is composed of various components that contribute to the overall capital structure of an investment. This section explores the key components of the private equity capital stack, including equity investments, debt investments, hybrid instruments, and other capital sources. It also highlights the order of payment and priority within the capital stack.

1. **Equity investments** are a primary component of the capital stack and include *common equity* and *preferred equity*.
    1. *Common equity* represents ownership in the investment and entitles investors to a share of the profits and potential appreciation in the value of the asset.
    2. *Preferred equity*, on the other hand, provides investors with certain preferential rights, such as priority in distributions and liquidation proceeds, before common equity holders. Preferred equity offers a greater level of security compared to common equity.
2. **Debt investments** are another key component of the capital stack. They involve providing financing to the investment through various debt instruments.
    1. *Senior debt* is the highest-ranking debt in the capital stack and holds priority in repayment. It is typically secured by the underlying assets and has lower interest rates compared to other forms of debt.
    2. *Mezzanine financing*, also known as mezzanine debt, falls between senior debt and equity. It is subordinated to senior debt but has a higher risk profile and potentially higher returns.
    3. *Subordinated debt* ranks below senior debt and mezzanine financing in terms of repayment priority.

Hybrid instruments are a combination of debt and equity characteristics. These instruments offer flexibility for investors to participate in potential equity appreciation while providing downside protection through the debt component.

1. **Convertible debt** allows the lender to convert the debt into equity at a specified conversion price and time.
2. **Warrants and options** provide the right to purchase equity at a predetermined price within a specified period.

Other capital sources may include **grants, government subsidies**, and **tax credits**. These sources provide additional funds to support the investment and can enhance the overall capital structure. Grants and subsidies are often provided by government entities or organizations to promote specific activities, such as community development or renewable energy projects. Tax credits, on the other hand, offer tax incentives to investors as a means to support certain types of investments.

The order of payment and priority within the capital stack is crucial in determining the repayment hierarchy in case of default or liquidation. Senior debt holders have the highest priority and are first in line to receive payment. They are followed by mezzanine debt, preferred equity, and common equity. The lower down the capital stack an investor is, the *higher the risk* they face, but also the potential for *greater returns*.

In summary, the private equity capital stack comprises equity investments, debt investments, hybrid instruments, and other capital sources. Each component has its characteristics and plays a distinct role in the capital structure. The order of payment and priority within the capital stack determines the repayment hierarchy in case of default or liquidation. Understanding these components and their order of priority is essential for investors to evaluate risk, structure investments, and make informed decisions in private equity endeavors.

4.3 Risk and Return Profiles in the Capital Stack

In the capital stack of private equity investments, risk and return profiles vary across the different components. This section focuses on the risk assessment and allocation across capital stack components, the relationship between risk and expected return, evaluating yield and potential upside in different capital stack layers, subordination and security in debt investments, and balancing risk and reward in capital stack composition.

Risk assessment and allocation play a crucial role in the capital stack. Each component of the capital stack carries its own risk profile, which determines its position and priority in the repayment hierarchy. Investors must assess the risk associated with each layer and allocate capital accordingly to achieve a balanced and diversified portfolio.

The relationship between risk and expected return is a fundamental principle in finance. Generally, higher-risk investments are expected to deliver higher returns, while lower-risk investments offer lower returns. In the capital stack, the layers that are higher up in the hierarchy, such as common equity and mezzanine financing, typically entail higher risk but also the potential for greater returns. Conversely, lower layers in the stack, such as senior debt and preferred equity, tend to have lower risk but also lower potential returns.

Evaluating yield and potential upside is essential when analyzing different layers of the capital stack. Debt investments, such as senior debt and mezzanine financing, often have predetermined interest rates that determine the yield for investors. The potential upside for equity investments, including common equity and preferred equity, is usually tied to the performance of the underlying asset and its ability to generate profits or appreciation in value.

Subordination and security are critical considerations in debt investments within the capital stack. Senior debt holders have a higher position in the repayment hierarchy and greater security because their claims are secured by the underlying assets. Mezzanine financing and subordinated debt, on the other hand, have lower priority and are considered subordinate to senior debt. These layers offer higher potential returns but also carry higher risk due to their subordinated position.

Balancing risk and reward is a key factor in determining the composition of the capital stack. Investors must strike a balance between higher-risk, higher-return components and lower-risk, lower-return components to achieve a diversified and well-structured portfolio. The allocation of capital across different layers should align with the investor's risk appetite, investment objectives, and overall investment strategy.

In summary, the risk and return profiles in the capital stack of private equity investments vary across different components. Investors need to assess and allocate risk across these components, considering the relationship between risk and expected return. Evaluating the yield and potential upside in different layers of the capital stack helps investors make informed decisions. Subordination and security are important considerations in debt investments, and balancing risk and reward is crucial in determining the composition of the capital stack. By understanding and managing the risk and return profiles within the capital stack, investors can optimize their investment strategies and enhance their chances of achieving their desired investment outcomes.

4.4 Interactions and Dynamics within the Capital Stack

The capital stack in private equity investments involves interactions and dynamics that influence deal negotiations and the rights and protections of different capital providers. This section explores the impact of capital stack structure on deal negotiations, the rights and protections for various capital providers, inter-creditor agreements and subordination agreements, and debt coverage ratios and loan-to-value ratios.

The structure of the capital stack can significantly impact deal negotiations. The positioning of different capital providers within the stack determines their *rights, priorities,* and *potential returns.* Equity investors, such as common equity holders and preferred equity investors, typically have more control and influence over the investment due to their higher position in the capital stack. Debt providers, on the other hand, may have more restrictive terms and protections to secure their repayment. The negotiation process takes into account these dynamics to strike a balance between the interests of various stakeholders.

Different capital providers in the capital stack have specific **rights and protections**. Debt providers, particularly senior debt holders, often have priority in repayment and may have additional protections, such as *security interests* in the underlying assets. Preferred equity investors may have *preferential rights to distributions* and liquidation proceeds. Common equity holders generally have *residual rights* and are entitled to a share of the profits and appreciation in the investment.

Intercreditor agreements and subordination agreements play a significant role in managing the interactions within the capital stack. These agreements outline the rights, priorities, and obligations of different capital providers.

1. *Intercreditor agreements* define the relationship between senior debt holders and subordinate debt holders, ensuring clear guidelines for repayment and enforcement actions.
2. *Subordination agreements* establish the order of payment within the capital stack, specifying the priority of claims in

case of default or liquidation.

Debt coverage ratios and loan-to-value ratios are important metrics used in evaluating the dynamics within the capital stack. Debt coverage ratio measures the ability of the investment to generate sufficient cash flow to cover debt service obligations. It provides an indication of the risk associated with debt repayment. Loan-to-value ratio assesses the percentage of the investment's value that is financed by debt.

In summary, the capital stack in private equity investments involves interactions and dynamics that impact deal negotiations and the rights and protections of capital providers. Understanding the impact of capital stack structure, the rights and protections for different providers, intercreditor agreements, debt coverage ratios, and loan-to-value ratios is crucial. By comprehending these interactions and dynamics, investors can make informed decisions and optimize the structure of their capital stack for successful investment outcomes.

4.5 Strategies for Optimizing the Capital Stack

Strategies for optimizing the capital stack in private equity investments involve determining the ideal capital stack structure for specific investments, balancing risk and return through capital stack composition, identifying the most cost-effective capital sources, accessing capital from various sources, and adjusting the capital stack to align with investment objectives and market conditions.

Determining the ideal capital stack structure for specific investments requires a careful assessment of the investment's characteristics, risk profile, and expected returns. Factors such as the *type of project*, *industry dynamics*, and *market conditions* play a significant role in determining the appropriate mix of debt and equity financing. For instance, a project with stable cash flows and lower risk may be better suited for a higher proportion of debt financing, while a growth-oriented project with higher risk may require a larger equity component.

Balancing risk and return through capital stack composition involves considering the *risk appetite* of the investor, *market conditions*, and the desired level of *potential returns*. Allocating capital across different layers of the capital stack can help diversify risk and enhance the overall portfolio performance.

Identifying the most cost-effective capital sources is crucial in optimizing the capital stack. This involves assessing various financing options, such as *banks, institutional investors, mezzanine lenders*, and other sources of capital. Each source may have different terms, interest rates, and requirements. Evaluating the costs and benefits of each source helps investors select the most favorable and cost-effective options, minimizing financing costs and maximizing returns.

Accessing capital from various sources is another strategy for optimizing the capital stack. By diversifying the sources of capital, investors can *reduce reliance on a single provider* and tap into different funding channels. This can *enhance flexibility, increase negotiating power*, and provide access to specialized expertise or unique financing structures. Building relationships with banks, institutional investors, and other capital providers enables investors to leverage a broader range of funding opportunities.

Adjusting the capital stack to align with investment objectives and market conditions is essential to adapt to changing circumstances. Market conditions, such as *interest rate fluctuations* or *shifts in investor preferences*, may necessitate adjustments to the capital structure. For example, during a period of low interest rates, it may be advantageous to increase debt financing to take advantage of lower borrowing costs. Regularly reviewing and adjusting the capital stack helps optimize the financing structure and align it with investment goals.

In summary, optimizing the capital stack in private equity investments involves determining the ideal structure, balancing risk and return, identifying cost-effective capital sources, accessing capital from various providers, and adjusting the stack to align with investment objectives and market conditions. By employing these strategies, investors can maximize returns, minimize costs, and enhance the overall performance of their investment portfolio.

Conclusion

In conclusion, a thorough understanding of the private equity capital stack and its analysis is crucial for effective investment management in the real estate industry. By comprehending the key concepts and terminologies related to the capital stack, investors can assess risk, allocate capital strategically, and optimize their financing strategies to achieve their investment objectives. Capital stack analysis is a fundamental tool in private equity investments, enabling investors to make informed decisions and maximize returns while managing risk effectively.

Chapter 5: Raising Capital for Private Equity Real Estate Funds

Presentation - Photo by Product School

5.1 Understanding the Capital Raising Process

Capital raising is a critical process for private equity real estate funds, as it provides the necessary funds to execute investment strategies and achieve fund objectives. Understanding the capital raising process is essential for fund managers to attract investors, secure commitments, and ensure the success of the fund. This section provides an introduction to capital raising for private equity real estate funds, emphasizes its importance, discusses the timeline and process, and highlights the legal and regulatory considerations involved.

Effective capital raising is crucial for the success of private equity real estate funds. It **provides the necessary capital** to acquire properties, implement value-add strategies, and generate returns for investors. Moreover, a robust capital base allows fund managers to take advantage of investment opportunities, diversify portfolios, and achieve economies of scale. By effectively raising capital, fund managers can build investor confidence, enhance their reputation, and attract new investors for future funds.

The capital raising process typically follows a timeline and involves several key steps.

1. Initially, fund managers must **identify the target capital amount and fund size** based on their investment strategy and market opportunities. This involves assessing the investment landscape, conducting market research, and considering the expected size of potential deals. Defining the target capital amount is crucial for setting fundraising goals and determining the scale of operations.

2. Once the target capital amount is established, fund managers embark on the **capital raising process**. This involves *identifying and approaching potential investors, conducting due diligence and qualification processes*, and *presenting the fund's investment thesis and track record*. Fund managers must effectively communicate the fund's value proposition, investment strategy, and expected returns to attract investor interest and secure commitments. This may involve creating a *compelling pitch deck, marketing materials*, and *holding meetings* with potential investors.

3. **Legal and regulatory considerations** play a significant role in the capital raising process. Fund managers must comply with *securities laws* and *regulations* governing the offering and sale of securities to investors. This includes ensuring proper documentation, such as private placement memorandums (PPMs), subscription agreements, and investor disclosures. Fund managers will need to *engage legal counsel* to navigate the regulatory landscape and ensure compliance with relevant regulations and investor protection measures.

In summary, effective capital raising is essential for the success of private equity real estate funds. By following a well-defined process, fund managers can identify the target capital amount, attract investors, and secure commitments. Legal and regulatory considerations are integral to the capital raising process, requiring compliance with securities laws and regulations. By understanding and effectively executing the capital raising process, fund managers can build a strong capital base, attract investors, and position the fund for success in the competitive real estate market.

5.2 Creating a Compelling Fund Strategy and Value Proposition

Creating a compelling fund strategy and value proposition is a crucial step in the capital raising process for private equity real estate funds. A well-defined investment strategy and a unique value proposition are essential to attract potential investors, differentiate the fund from competitors, and align with market opportunities. This section explores the key considerations in developing a compelling fund strategy and value proposition, including defining the investment strategy and focus, developing a unique value proposition, identifying competitive advantages, crafting the investment thesis and targeted returns, and aligning the strategy with investor preferences and market opportunities.

1. **Defining the fund's investment strategy and focus** is the foundation of a compelling fund strategy. Fund managers need to clearly articulate the types of real estate assets they intend to invest in, such as *residential*, *commercial*, or *industrial properties*, and identify the geographic regions or markets they will target. This strategic decision helps investors understand the fund's expertise and investment objectives. Furthermore, it enables the fund manager to

allocate resources effectively, develop a track record in specific sectors or regions, and capitalize on market opportunities.

2. **Developing a unique value proposition** is critical to *differentiate the fund* from competitors and attract investors. The value proposition should clearly articulate the fund's *unique selling points* and the *benefits* investors can expect. This can include factors such as the fund manager's experience and track record, the fund's access to exclusive deal flow, a specialized investment strategy, or a unique approach to value creation. A compelling value proposition helps investors understand why they should choose the fund over other investment options and highlights the fund's competitive advantages.

3. **Identifying the fund's competitive advantages** is another important aspect of creating a compelling fund strategy. This involves assessing the *strengths and weaknesses* of the fund manager and the fund's *investment approach*. Competitive advantages can include factors such as *deep industry knowledge, strong relationships with industry players,* a *proven track record of successful investments,* a *differentiated investment process,* or *access to proprietary market information.* Identifying and leveraging these advantages is essential in positioning the fund as an attractive investment opportunity.

4. **Crafting the fund's investment thesis and targeted returns** is a key element of the value proposition. The investment thesis outlines the fund's *fundamental beliefs about the market* and *investment opportunities* and how it intends to generate attractive returns for investors. It should include a clear articulation of the fund's investment strategy, the rationale behind it, and the expected outcomes. Additionally, the fund should establish *targeted returns* that are realistic and achievable, considering factors such as the risk profile, market

conditions, and investor expectations.

5. Lastly, **aligning the fund's strategy with investor preferences and market opportunities** is crucial. Fund managers need to understand the preferences and requirements of their target investors, such as their *risk appetite*, *return expectations*, and *investment horizons*. By aligning the fund's strategy with these preferences, fund managers can attract investors who are a good fit for the fund and increase the likelihood of capital commitments. Additionally, staying abreast of market opportunities and trends allows fund managers to position the fund to capitalize on emerging opportunities and meet investor demand.

In conclusion, creating a compelling fund strategy and value proposition is essential for successful capital raising in private equity real estate funds. Defining the investment strategy, developing a unique value proposition, identifying competitive advantages, crafting the investment thesis and targeted returns, and aligning the strategy with investor preferences and market opportunities are all critical elements of this process. By effectively communicating the fund's value proposition and aligning it with investor needs and market dynamics, fund managers can attract capital and position their fund for success in the competitive landscape of private equity real estate.

5.3 SEC Regulations for raising capital for Private Equity Real Estate Fund

Raising capital for private equity real estate funds involves compliance with Securities and Exchange Commission (SEC) regulations. Understanding these regulations is crucial for fund managers seeking to raise capital, as non-compliance can lead to legal and financial consequences. This section provides an overview of SEC regulations, offering exemptions, Regulation D (Rule 506), Regulation A, SEC filing and reporting requirements, investor protection, and the importance of legal counsel and compliance.

The *SEC is a regulatory agency* that oversees the securities industry in the United States. Its role is to protect investors, maintain fair and efficient markets, and facilitate capital formation. Private equity real estate fund managers are subject to SEC regulations as they offer and sell securities to investors. Compliance with these regulations is vital to ensure transparency, fairness, and investor protection.

To facilitate capital raising, the SEC provides **exemptions** that private equity real estate fund managers can utilize. The most commonly used exemptions include Regulation D (Rule 506) and Regulation A.

1. **Regulation D** allows fund managers to offer and sell securities without registering with the SEC, provided certain conditions are met. It has two distinct offerings: *Rule 506(b)* allows the offering to a limited number of non-accredited investors, while *Rule 506(c)* permits the offering to accredited investors only and allows general solicitation and advertising.
2. **Regulation A**, also known as the "mini-IPO" exemption, allows private equity real estate fund managers to conduct *public offerings* of securities up to a certain limit. It offers a streamlined process for *smaller offerings* and provides an opportunity to reach a wider investor base. However, it involves additional filing and reporting requirements compared to Regulation D offerings.

Fund managers must comply with SEC filing and reporting obligations when raising capital.

1. For offerings conducted under *Regulation D*, fund managers are required to file Form D with the SEC and provide specified information about the offering. Ongoing *reporting obligations* may also apply.
2. *Regulation A* offerings require more comprehensive and periodic reporting to provide investors with detailed information about the fund's operations and financials.

The SEC places great emphasis on **investor protection** and enforces anti-fraud provisions. Fund managers must ensure that they provide accurate and complete information to investors, avoid making misleading statements, and follow proper disclosure practices. Adhering to these principles helps maintain investor trust and credibility, while protecting against fraudulent activities.

Engaging experienced legal counsel is crucial for private equity real estate fund managers to navigate SEC regulations. Legal professionals with expertise in securities laws can provide *guidance on compliance requirements*, assist in *structuring offerings*, and ensure *proper disclosure practices*. Additionally, compliance officers play a vital role within private equity real estate firms, overseeing adherence to SEC regulations and implementing internal controls to mitigate legal and regulatory risks.

In conclusion, understanding and complying with SEC regulations is essential for private equity real estate fund managers when raising capital. Adhering to these regulations allows fund managers to navigate the capital raising process effectively, maintain investor trust, and mitigate legal and regulatory risks associated with securities offerings. Engaging experienced legal counsel and having robust compliance practices are instrumental in ensuring compliance with SEC regulations throughout the capital raising process.

5.4 Accredited versus non-accredited Investors

Accredited and non-accredited investors play different roles in private equity real estate investments due to regulatory requirements. This section provides an overview of the definition and criteria for accredited investors, the benefits and privileges they enjoy, limitations for non-accredited investors, investor protection, and disclosure requirements. It also touches upon evolving regulations and potential changes to the accredited investor definition.

Accredited investors are individuals or entities that meet certain **income or net worth thresholds** defined by securities regulations. The criteria for accreditation may include having an *annual income* exceeding a certain threshold (e.g., $200,000 for individuals or $300,000 for couples) or a *net worth* exceeding a specified amount (e.g., $1 million excluding the value of a primary residence). Accredited investors are deemed to have sufficient *financial sophistication* and resources to bear the risks associated with certain private equity real estate investments.

Accredited investors enjoy **benefits and privileges** in accessing a wider range of investment opportunities. They have the flexibility to participate in *private placements, hedge funds*, and other *alternative investments* that may not be available to non-accredited investors. These investments often have *higher potential returns* and offer *diversification* beyond traditional investment options. Accredited investors have the opportunity to allocate a portion of their portfolio to alternative assets, which can enhance their investment strategies and potentially generate higher long-term gains.

On the other hand, **non-accredited investors** may face *limitations due to regulatory requirements*. The regulations aim to protect these investors from potentially higher-risk investments that may not be suitable for their financial situation. Non-accredited investors may have *restricted access* to certain private equity real estate investments, such as *private placements* or investments with *higher minimum investment thresholds*. The limitations are in place to ensure that non-accredited investors are not exposed to undue risk or investments that may be beyond their financial capabilities.

Investor protection and disclosure requirements are crucial elements of securities regulations. When dealing with non-accredited investors, issuers of private equity real estate investments are obligated to provide comprehensive disclosures and information. These requirements aim to ensure *transparency*, enable *informed investment decisions*, and *protect the interests of non-accredited investors*. The disclosures typically cover investment objectives, risks, fees, past performance, and other material information that helps investors evaluate the investment opportunity.

In conclusion, the distinction between accredited and non-accredited investors is based on regulatory criteria that determine eligibility to participate in certain private equity real estate investments. Accredited investors enjoy benefits such as wider investment opportunities and potentially higher returns. Non-accredited investors face limitations aimed at protecting them from higher-risk investments. Investor protection and disclosure requirements are essential elements of regulatory oversight. As regulations evolve, changes to the accredited investor definition may impact both accredited and non-accredited investors in terms of their access to private equity real estate investments and the investment landscape.

5.5 Documents required for Private Equity fund raising

When engaging in private equity fund raising, certain essential documents are required to convey information, establish legal frameworks, and outline the terms and conditions of the investment. This section provides an overview of the key documents involved in private equity fund raising and emphasizes their importance in presenting investment opportunities and ensuring legal compliance.

The offering memorandum (OM) is a comprehensive document provided to potential investors. It serves as the primary source of information about the fund, detailing the *investment strategy, target markets, track record, fees and expenses, risk factors*, and other relevant disclosures. The OM plays a crucial role in presenting the fund's value proposition and investment opportunity in a clear, accurate, and compelling manner.

The subscription agreement is a legal document through which investors make their investment commitments. It outlines the terms and conditions of the investment, including the *investment amount, payment terms, representations and warranties*, and *investor eligibility*. Subscription agreements need to be carefully reviewed and customized to ensure compliance with applicable laws and regulations.

The limited partnership agreement (LPA) governs the rights, obligations, and governance structure of the fund. LPAs include provisions related to *profit allocation, management fees, voting rights, withdrawal rights*, and *dissolution provisions*. Legal counsel plays a vital role in drafting and negotiating LPAs to protect the interests of both the general partner and limited partners.

Confidentiality agreements, also known as *non-disclosure agreements (NDAs)*, are used to protect sensitive information shared with potential investors during the fund raising process. These agreements help safeguard proprietary information and maintain investor trust by ensuring that the shared information remains confidential.

Fundraising documents should also include necessary compliance and regulatory disclosures. **Anti-money laundering (AML) requirements, know-your-customer (KYC) procedures**, and other regulatory disclosures as required by applicable laws and regulations need to be incorporated to ensure compliance with legal and regulatory obligations.

The importance of **legal counsel and compliance officers** cannot be overstated when it comes to reviewing and preparing fundraising documents. Their expertise and attention to detail are crucial in ensuring the completeness, accuracy, and compliance of these documents with applicable securities laws and regulations.

By presenting investment opportunities in a professional and legally compliant manner, private equity firms can instill confidence in potential investors and increase the likelihood of successful fundraising efforts. The completeness and accuracy of fundraising documents are vital for establishing trust, attracting investors, and complying with legal and regulatory requirements.

5.6 Building Relationships with Limited Partners (LPs)

Building strong relationships with limited partners (LPs) is a critical aspect of private equity fundraising. This section focuses on key strategies and considerations for cultivating and maintaining relationships with LPs.

1. The first step in building relationships with LPs is to **identify and target potential investors** who align with the fund's investment strategy and objectives. This involves conducting *market research and leveraging industry networks* to identify LPs who have a history of investing in similar types of funds or have shown interest in the fund's target sector or geography.
2. Once potential LPs have been identified, the fund manager should **approach and engage with them** in a thoughtful and strategic manner. This involves crafting a *compelling value*

proposition that highlights the fund's investment strategy, track record, and potential for returns. *Building rapport* with LPs through personalized communication, such as one-on-one meetings and tailored presentations, is crucial in establishing a foundation for a mutually beneficial relationship.

3. **Conducting due diligence on potential LPs** is an important step to assess their suitability as investors. This may involve evaluating their financial stability, investment preferences, and alignment with the fund's objectives. Thorough due diligence helps ensure that the *LP's investment goals align* with the fund's strategy and that they can provide the necessary capital and support.

4. **Crafting effective investor presentations and pitch decks** is essential for conveying the fund's *investment thesis, strategy,* and *track record.* These materials should be clear, concise, and tailored to the specific needs and preferences of the LP. Highlighting the fund's *unique value proposition, competitive advantage,* and *potential for returns* is crucial in capturing the interest and attention of potential LPs.

5. **Nurturing long-term relationships** with existing and prospective LPs is vital for fund success. This involves maintaining *regular communication,* providing *timely updates* on the fund's performance and investment activities, and *seeking feedback* from LPs. Fund managers should also prioritize transparency and trust by providing accurate and comprehensive information and addressing any investor concerns or inquiries promptly.

By identifying and targeting potential LPs, approaching them strategically, conducting due diligence, crafting compelling presentations, and nurturing relationships over time, fund managers can build strong partnerships with LPs. These relationships not only support successful fundraising efforts but also contribute to long-term investor loyalty, potential future investments, and a positive reputation within the private equity industry.

5.7 Fund Marketing and Investor Communication

Fund marketing and investor communication are crucial components of successful fundraising and maintaining strong relationships with investors. This section explores key strategies and considerations in fund marketing and investor communication.

Developing a comprehensive fund marketing plan is essential to effectively reach and attract potential investors. This involves defining *target investor profiles*, outlining *marketing objectives*, and identifying the most suitable *marketing channels and platforms*. The plan should also include a clear messaging strategy that highlights the fund's unique value proposition and investment strategy.

Leveraging digital marketing channels and platforms can significantly enhance the reach and visibility of a fund. This includes *utilizing websites, social media platforms, email marketing*, and *online advertising* to engage with potential investors. Implementing effective *search engine optimization (SEO)* techniques and creating compelling content such as *blog posts, articles*, and *videos* can help build credibility and attract qualified leads.

Organizing investor meetings, roadshows, and conferences provides opportunities for fund managers to *engage with potential investors in person*. These events allow for *direct interaction, presentation of investment opportunities*, and *answering investor questions*. Roadshows, in particular, involve traveling to different cities or regions to meet with interested investors and provide them with comprehensive information about the fund.

Crafting marketing collateral and fund documents that effectively communicate the fund's investment strategy, track record, and potential returns is essential. These materials may include the fund's *offering memorandum, pitch decks, fact sheets,* and *brochures.* It is important to ensure that these documents are professionally designed, accurately represent the fund's offerings, and adhere to applicable regulatory requirements.

Establishing ongoing investor communication and reporting protocols is vital to maintaining *transparency* and *building trust* with investors. Regular communication can include periodic *newsletters, performance updates,* and *investor reports.* Fund managers should provide comprehensive and timely information about the fund's performance, portfolio updates, and market insights to keep investors informed and engaged.

By developing a comprehensive fund marketing plan, leveraging digital marketing channels, organizing investor meetings and conferences, crafting compelling marketing collateral, and establishing ongoing investor communication protocols, fund managers can effectively promote their fund, attract potential investors, and maintain strong relationships with existing investors. These efforts contribute to a successful fundraising process and foster long-term investor satisfaction and loyalty.

5.8 Negotiating Terms and Structuring Limited Partner Agreements

Negotiating terms and structuring limited partner agreements are crucial aspects of the private equity fund-raising process. This section explores the key considerations and steps involved in this process.

Limited partner agreements (LPAs) outline the **terms and conditions** between the fund manager (general partner) and the limited partners.

It is essential to carefully negotiate and define key terms, such as the fund's *duration, investment strategy, management fees, carried interest, profit-sharing arrangements, reporting requirements,* and *governance structure.* These terms should align with the fund's objectives and investor expectations.

Negotiating fund terms, fee structures, and profit-sharing arrangements requires a thorough understanding of **investor preferences and industry standards.** Fund managers should consider factors such as the *size of the fund, investment strategy, track record, risk profile,* and *competitive landscape* when determining the appropriate fee structure and profit-sharing mechanisms. Balancing the interests of both the fund manager and the limited partners is crucial to reaching mutually beneficial terms.

Compliance and regulatory considerations play a significant role in fund structuring. Fund managers must ensure compliance with relevant *securities laws, regulatory requirements,* and *industry standards.* This includes adhering to *anti-money laundering (AML)* regulations, *know-your-customer (KYC)* procedures, and other legal and regulatory obligations. Engaging legal counsel and compliance professionals is essential to navigate the complex regulatory landscape and mitigate potential risks.

Documenting and finalizing limited partner agreements require meticulous attention to detail and legal expertise. The LPAs should accurately reflect the *negotiated terms, investor preferences,* and *regulatory requirements.* Drafting clear and comprehensive agreements, conducting thorough legal reviews, and addressing any concerns or questions from the limited partners are critical steps in finalizing the agreements.

By carefully negotiating terms and structuring limited partner agreements, fund managers can establish a solid foundation for the fund's operations and investor relationships. This involves understanding investor preferences, considering industry standards, complying with regulatory requirements, and documenting the agreements accurately. A well-structured and mutually beneficial limited partner agreement enhances transparency, aligns investor expectations, and fosters a successful and long-lasting partnership between the fund manager and the limited partners.

Conclusion

Raising capital for private equity real estate funds is a critical process that significantly impacts the success of the fund. In this section, we have explored key concepts and strategies involved in this process.

In conclusion, the capital raising process is a complex endeavor that requires strategic planning, legal compliance, effective communication, and relationship-building. By understanding the key concepts and implementing appropriate strategies, fund managers can increase their chances of successfully raising capital for private equity real estate funds and achieving their investment objectives.

Chapter 6: Evaluating Real Estate Investment Opportunities

Evaluation - Photo by Chris Liverani

6.1 Introduction to Real Estate Investment Evaluation

In this section, we will provide an introduction to real estate investment evaluation. We will emphasize the significance of thorough evaluation in Private Equity Real Estate (PERE) investments and provide an overview of the investment evaluation process. Lastly, we will explore the importance of establishing evaluation criteria and investment objectives for effective decision-making.

Real Estate Investment Evaluation is a critical process that plays a pivotal role in Private Equity Real Estate (PERE) investments.

1. **Thorough evaluation** is of paramount importance in this field, as it allows investors to assess the potential risks and returns associated with real estate investments. By carefully analyzing key factors and employing due diligence, investors

can make informed decisions and maximize their investment outcomes.

2. When it comes to real estate investment evaluation, **several key factors need to be considered**. These factors include the *location of the property*, *market conditions*, *property type*, *cash flow projections*, *financing options*, and potential *exit strategies*. Evaluating the location is crucial since it determines the property's proximity to amenities, transportation hubs, and economic centers. Market conditions, such as supply and demand dynamics and price trends, provide insights into the property's growth potential and liquidity. Property type also affects the evaluation, as different asset classes have varying risk profiles and potential for appreciation.

3. The **investment evaluation process** ensures that all relevant information is gathered, potential risks are identified, and the investment's viability is assessed. The process involves the following high-level stages.

    1. Initially, investors *identify potential investment opportunities* based on their investment objectives and evaluation criteria. These criteria typically include factors such as *target return rates*, *risk tolerance*, *investment horizon*, and *asset class preferences*.

    2. Once opportunities are identified, *due diligence* plays a crucial role. It involves conducting a comprehensive analysis of the property, including *legal*, *financial*, and *physical inspections*.

4. To establish evaluation criteria and investment objectives, investors need to **define their goals and preferences**. This includes determining the desired *return on investment*, *acceptable risk levels*, and *investment holding period*. Evaluation criteria may also encompass factors like the

property's potential for *rental income*, potential for *value appreciation*, and alignment with the investor's *long-term strategy*. By clearly defining these criteria and objectives, investors can streamline the evaluation process and focus on opportunities that align with their goals.

In conclusion, real estate investment evaluation is a crucial aspect of PERE investments. Thorough evaluation allows investors to assess risks and returns associated with potential investments, enabling them to make informed decisions. Key factors such as location, market conditions, and property type play significant roles in this process. The investment evaluation process involves stages like identifying opportunities, conducting due diligence, and analyzing the gathered information. By establishing evaluation criteria and investment objectives, investors can streamline the evaluation process and increase their chances of success in the real estate market.

6.2 Market Analysis and Feasibility Assessment

In this section, we will focus on market analysis and feasibility assessment in real estate investment. We will delve into the process of conducting thorough market research and analysis and explore the evaluation of market cycles and economic factors that can impact investment decisions. Furthermore, we will discuss the importance of analyzing comparable sales and rental rates to gauge the market's potential. Lastly, we will highlight the significance of determining market feasibility and growth potential for successful real estate investments.

Market analysis and feasibility assessment are essential components of real estate investment evaluation.

By **conducting thorough market research and analysis**, investors can gain insights into *market trends, supply and demand dynamics*, and *assess the feasibility and growth potential* of their investment. Market research involves gathering and analyzing data related to the real estate market. This includes studying *demographic information, economic indicators,* and *local regulations.* Investors need to understand the market dynamics, such as *population growth, employment rates,* and *income levels,* as these factors influence the demand for real estate properties. Additionally, analyzing local regulations and zoning laws helps determine the potential for future development and the impact on property values.

Assessing market trends is crucial to identify opportunities and risks. Investors need to analyze factors like *property price trends, rental rates,* and *vacancy rates.* This analysis provides insights into the overall *health of the market* and helps determine the potential for *rental income* and *property appreciation.* Understanding supply and demand dynamics is also essential. Investors need to assess the current and projected supply of properties in the market and compare it with the demand to identify potential imbalances and opportunities.

Evaluating market cycles and economic factors is another important aspect of market analysis. Real estate markets are cyclical, experiencing periods of growth, stability, and decline. By studying historical market cycles and economic indicators, investors can anticipate potential market fluctuations and adjust their investment strategies accordingly. Economic factors such as *interest rates, inflation,* and *GDP growth* also impact the real estate market.

Analyzing comparable sales and rental rates is crucial for determining property values and potential rental income. By examining recent *sales of similar properties in the area,* investors can estimate the market value of the property they are evaluating. Similarly, analyzing rental rates for comparable properties helps determine the *potential rental income* and yield of the investment. These comparisons provide a benchmark for evaluating the investment's financial feasibility and its attractiveness relative to other properties in the market.

Ultimately, market feasibility and growth potential assessment are vital steps in real estate investment evaluation. By conducting thorough market research and analysis, investors can make informed decisions based on the current and projected market conditions. This analysis helps determine the viability and potential returns of the investment, enabling investors to maximize their chances of success in the real estate market.

6.3 Financial Analysis and Investment Modeling

In this section, we will delve into financial analysis and investment modeling in the realm of real estate. We will explore the process of analyzing property financials and performance history, the evaluation of return metrics, and the sensitivity analysis and risk assessment. Lastly, we will highlight the importance of creating investment models and performing scenario analysis to make informed investment decisions.

Financial analysis and investment modeling are crucial components of real estate investment evaluation. By analyzing *property financials*, conducting *cash flow analysis*, evaluating *return metrics*, performing *sensitivity analysis*, and creating *investment models*, investors can assess the financial viability and potential risks associated with their investment.

1. Analyzing **property financials** and performance history is an important step in understanding the current and past financial performance of a property. Investors examine factors such as *rental income, operating expenses, debt service,* and *vacancy rates*. This analysis helps identify any potential

issues or opportunities and provides a clear picture of the property's financial health.

2. Conducting **cash flow analysis** and projections is essential for evaluating the investment's potential returns. Investors estimate the expected cash inflows and outflows over the investment period, taking into account factors such as *rental income, operating expenses, debt payments*, and potential *capital expenditures*. By projecting cash flows, investors can assess the property's ability to generate positive cash flow and determine its potential profitability.

3. Evaluating **return metrics** is a critical aspect of financial analysis. Common return metrics used in real estate investments include the *capitalization rate (cap rate), cash-on-cash return*, and *internal rate of return (IRR)*.

    1. The *cap rate* provides a measure of the property's expected annual return based on its purchase price.

    2. *Cash-on-cash return* compares the property's annual cash flow to the initial investment.

    3. *IRR* calculates the compound annual rate of return over the investment period, considering both cash inflows and outflows. These metrics help investors assess the potential returns and compare different investment opportunities.

4. **Sensitivity analysis** and **risk assessment** are important in evaluating the investment's robustness against various scenarios. Investors analyze how changes in variables like *rental income, expenses*, and *interest rates* impact the investment's financial performance. This analysis helps identify potential risks and assess the investment's sensitivity to market fluctuations.

5. Creating **investment models** and performing **scenario analysis** allows investors to evaluate the impact of different

factors on the investment's financial outcomes. By building financial models, investors can simulate various scenarios and assess the potential risks and rewards. This analysis helps in making informed decisions and identifying the optimal investment strategy.

In conclusion, financial analysis and investment modeling are essential in real estate investment evaluation. By analyzing property financials, conducting cash flow analysis, evaluating return metrics, performing sensitivity analysis, and creating investment models, investors can assess the financial viability and risks associated with their investments. These analyses provide insights into the investment's potential returns, its sensitivity to market changes, and help in making informed investment decisions.

6.4 Property Due Diligence and Risk Assessment

Property due diligence and risk assessment are critical components of real estate investment evaluation. By conducting thorough inspections, evaluating environmental factors, reviewing legal documentation, assessing zoning restrictions, and identifying potential liabilities, investors can mitigate risks and make informed decisions about their investments.

1. **Physical property inspection and condition assessment** involve conducting a detailed examination of the property's physical attributes and condition. This includes inspecting the *building's structure, systems*, and *components*, such as the roof, foundation, plumbing, electrical systems, and HVAC. The purpose of this inspection is to identify any potential issues or maintenance needs that may affect the property's value or require additional investment.
2. **Evaluating environmental factors and potential risks** is

crucial to assess any environmental hazards or liabilities associated with the property. This involves conducting *environmental assessments*, such as Phase I and Phase II environmental site assessments, to identify any potential contamination or risks. Environmental factors may include soil and groundwater contamination, presence of hazardous materials, or proximity to environmentally sensitive areas. By understanding these factors, investors can determine the potential impact on the property's value and any necessary remediation measures.

3. **Reviewing legal and title documentation** is essential to ensure a clear and marketable title. Investors need to examine *property deeds, title insurance policies, surveys,* and any *encumbrances or liens* on the property. This review helps identify any legal issues or restrictions that may affect the property's ownership or use. It is important to ensure that there are no outstanding legal disputes, zoning violations, or other legal challenges that could pose risks or impede the investment.

4. **Assessing zoning and land use restrictions** is necessary to understand the property's permitted uses and any limitations imposed by local regulations. Investors need to review *zoning ordinances, land use plans,* and any applicable *restrictions* or *variances.* This assessment helps determine whether the property aligns with the investor's intended use and whether there are any potential obstacles or limitations to consider.

5. **Identifying potential liabilities and developing mitigation strategies** is crucial to minimize risks associated with the investment. This involves identifying potential issues such as outstanding *tax liabilities, pending lawsuits,* or *lease disputes.* By identifying these liabilities, investors can develop appropriate mitigation strategies, such as negotiating

favorable lease terms, resolving outstanding legal issues, or obtaining appropriate insurance coverage.

In conclusion, property due diligence and risk assessment are integral parts of real estate investment evaluation. By conducting physical property inspections, evaluating environmental factors, reviewing legal documentation, assessing zoning restrictions, and identifying potential liabilities, investors can mitigate risks and make informed investment decisions. Thorough due diligence helps ensure that investors have a comprehensive understanding of the property and its associated risks, allowing them to maximize their chances of success in the real estate market.

6.5 Investment Structure and Deal Negotiation

Investment structure and deal negotiation are crucial aspects of real estate investment evaluation. By evaluating investment structures and tax considerations, negotiating purchase and sale agreements, structuring financing, addressing legal and regulatory compliance, and analyzing risk-reward tradeoffs, investors can optimize the terms of their investments and ensure compliance with applicable laws.

1. **Evaluating investment structures and tax considerations** involves assessing different legal and tax frameworks for real estate investments. Investors need to consider options such as *limited partnerships (LPs)* or *limited liability companies (LLCs)*. Each structure has its advantages and tax implications, and investors must carefully evaluate them to optimize their investment strategy and minimize tax liabilities.

2. **Negotiating purchase and sale agreements** is a crucial step in the investment process. Investors need to carefully review and negotiate the terms and conditions of the agreement,

including *purchase price, financing contingencies, inspection periods*, and *closing dates*. Skillful negotiation can help investors secure favorable terms and protect their interests during the transaction.

3. **Structuring financing and capital stack** involves determining the appropriate mix of debt and equity to fund the investment. Investors evaluate various financing options, such as *traditional bank loans, private lenders*, or *joint venture partnerships*. They also analyze the capital stack, which refers to the order of priority for different sources of capital. By structuring financing effectively, investors can optimize their returns and manage their financial risk.

4. **Addressing legal and regulatory compliance** is essential to ensure that the investment adheres to applicable laws and regulations. Investors need to navigate legal requirements related to *property ownership, leasing agreements, environmental regulations*, and any specific local or national regulations. By addressing compliance issues proactively, investors can mitigate legal risks and avoid potential penalties or disputes.

5. **Analyzing risk-reward tradeoffs and investment terms** involves assessing the potential returns against the associated risks. Investors evaluate factors such as the property's *income potential, market conditions, financing costs*, and *exit strategies*. They also analyze investment terms, including target returns, holding periods, and profit-sharing structures. This analysis helps investors make informed decisions about the risk-reward profile of the investment and negotiate favorable terms that align with their investment objectives.

In conclusion, investment structure and deal negotiation are critical components of real estate investment evaluation. By evaluating investment structures and tax considerations, negotiating purchase and sale agreements, structuring financing, addressing legal and regulatory compliance, and analyzing risk-reward tradeoffs, investors can optimize their investment terms and ensure compliance with applicable laws. These steps are crucial for creating a solid investment framework and maximizing the potential returns of real estate investments.

Conclusion

Thorough evaluation of real estate investment opportunities is essential for PERE firms to make informed decisions and achieve optimal outcomes. Key concepts include market analysis, financial analysis, due diligence, risk assessment, and investment structure. Market analysis provides insights into viability and growth prospects. Financial analysis and investment modeling assess financial feasibility and potential returns. Due diligence and risk assessment identify issues and mitigate risks. Investment structure and deal negotiation optimize terms and ensure compliance. By employing these concepts, PERE firms can navigate the real estate market, minimize risks, and maximize their chances of success.

Chapter 7: Investing in Private Equity Residential Real Estate

Residential - Photo by Ronnie George

7.1 Introduction to Private Equity Residential Real Estate

Private Equity Residential Real Estate refers to the investment activity in residential properties by private equity firms. It involves the acquisition, development, and management of residential properties with the objective of generating attractive returns for investors. This sector focuses on single-family homes, multi-family buildings, apartments, and other residential properties.

Residential real estate holds significant importance in private equity investments due to several reasons.

1. Firstly, residential properties offer **stable cash flows** through *rental income*, making them attractive assets for long-term investment.
2. Additionally, residential real estate is considered a tangible

asset with **inherent value**, providing a *sense of security* to investors.

3. The housing market also benefits from a **consistent demand for housing**, driven by population growth, urbanization, and changing demographics.

Residential real estate **differs from commercial real estate** in terms of usage and investor characteristics. Residential properties are primarily used for *housing purposes*, while commercial properties are utilized for *business operations*. Residential properties tend to have *smaller transaction sizes* and a larger pool of potential tenants or buyers. On the other hand, commercial properties are often subject to longer lease terms and higher capital requirements.

The residential real estate sector exhibits **promising market demand and growth potential**. Factors such as population growth, urban migration, and lifestyle preferences contribute to the *continuous demand* for housing. Moreover, demographic shifts, such as the rise of the millennial generation and the *aging population*, influence housing needs and create investment opportunities in different segments of the residential market. These dynamics make residential real estate an attractive sector for private equity investors seeking stable income streams and potential capital appreciation.

Private equity firms play a significant role in residential real estate investments. Their expertise in sourcing, analyzing, and executing real estate transactions allows them to identify *undervalued properties*, implement *value-add strategies*, and *optimize investment performance*. Private equity firms often leverage their network of industry professionals, including property managers and developers, to enhance the operational efficiency and profitability of residential properties. Additionally, private equity investments bring institutional capital to the residential real estate sector, enabling the development of new projects and the revitalization of existing properties.

In conclusion, private equity residential real estate encompasses investment activities in residential properties by private equity firms. It plays a vital role in the private equity investment landscape, offering stable cash flows, tangible assets, and long-term growth potential. Residential real estate distinguishes itself from commercial real estate through its usage, transaction sizes, and investor characteristics. With a consistent demand for housing and demographic trends driving the sector's growth, private equity firms contribute to the development and optimization of residential properties, generating attractive returns for investors.

7.2 Types of Residential Real Estate Investments

In this section, we will explore different types of residential real estate investments. We will discuss the opportunities presented by single-family homes, multifamily properties, student housing, senior housing, and vacation and short-term rental properties.

Residential real estate investments offer a diverse range of opportunities for private equity firms. Some of the common types of residential real estate investments include:

1. **Single-Family Homes:** This category includes the acquisition and management of individual houses. Private equity firms may focus on rental properties, where they purchase homes and lease them to tenants, generating a steady rental income. Alternatively, they may engage in *fix-and-flip projects*, purchasing distressed properties, renovating them, and selling them at a higher price.
2. **Multifamily Properties:** Multifamily properties consist of apartment buildings, condominiums buildings, and

townhouse complexes. Private equity firms can invest in the acquisition and management of these properties, which offer *multiple rental units* within a single complex. This allows for economies of scale in property management and provides a diversified income stream from multiple tenants.

3. **Student Housing:** This type of residential investment targets the housing needs of college and university students. It includes the development or *acquisition of dormitories* or *off-campus housing*. Private equity firms often collaborate with educational institutions or property management companies to cater to the specific needs of student tenants.

4. **Senior Housing:** Senior housing investments focus on providing housing solutions for older adults. This category includes *independent living communities*, *assisted living facilities*, and *memory care facilities*. Private equity firms may invest in the development or acquisition of these specialized properties, taking into account the growing demand driven by an aging population.

5. **Vacation and Short-Term Rental Properties:** This category involves the investment in properties that cater to vacationers and short-term renters. Private equity firms may acquire properties in desirable locations and offer them as vacation rentals or list them on platforms like Airbnb. This type of investment can generate attractive rental income.

It's worth noting that private equity firms may specialize in *one or more of these* residential real estate investment types, depending on their investment strategies and expertise. Each type of investment comes with its own considerations, such as *location, market demand, property management*, and *regulatory requirements*. Private equity firms employ rigorous due diligence and analysis to identify opportunities, optimize property performance, and generate attractive returns from their residential real estate investments.

7.3 Key Factors to Consider When Investing in Residential Real Estate

In this section, we will discuss the key factors to consider when investing in residential real estate. This includes analyzing location, rental market conditions, property management options, tenant profiles, and regulatory considerations.

When investing in residential real estate, several key factors need to be considered to make informed investment decisions. These factors include:

1. **Location Analysis:** Location plays a critical role in the success of residential real estate investments. Factors such as *demographics*, *market demand*, and *neighborhood dynamics* need to be carefully assessed. Understanding the target market's preferences, income levels, and population growth trends helps identify locations with strong rental demand and growth potential.

2. **Rental Market Analysis:** Conducting a thorough analysis of the rental market is crucial. This includes evaluating *rent levels* in the area, historical and current *occupancy rates*, and overall *rental demand*. This analysis provides insights into the income-generating potential of the property and helps determine appropriate rental rates to ensure competitiveness and profitability.

3. **Property Management Considerations:** Effective property management is essential for maximizing returns on residential real estate investments. Private equity firms need to decide whether to handle property management *in-house*

or *outsource* it to a third-party management company. Factors such as maintenance, tenant communication, rent collection, and property upkeep should be carefully considered to ensure smooth operations and tenant satisfaction.

4. **Tenant Profiles:** Identifying the target tenant segment is crucial for residential real estate investments. Understanding the preferences, needs, and demographics of the target market helps in *property marketing, tenant retention*, and overall *investment success*. Additionally, implementing a rigorous tenant screening process is vital to ensure reliable and responsible tenants who will uphold the property's value and pay rent on time.

5. **Regulatory and Legal Considerations:** Compliance with landlord-tenant laws and housing regulations is essential when investing in residential real estate. Investors must have a solid understanding of the *legal framework* governing rental properties in the target location. This includes knowledge of *eviction processes, tenant rights, lease agreements*, and other legal obligations to ensure full compliance and mitigate potential legal risks.

By considering these key factors, private equity firms can make well-informed decisions when investing in residential real estate. Thorough analysis of location, rental market dynamics, property management strategies, tenant profiles, and regulatory compliance helps mitigate risks and optimize investment returns. Additionally, staying updated with market trends and maintaining a proactive approach to property management ensures long-term success in the residential real estate sector.

7.4 Evaluating Residential Real Estate Opportunities

In this section, we will explore evaluating residential real estate opportunities through financial analysis, property condition assessment, market analysis, exit strategies, and financing considerations.

When evaluating residential real estate opportunities, several factors should be taken into account to *assess the investment potential.* These factors include:

1. **Financial Analysis:** Conducting a comprehensive financial analysis is crucial to understand the income-generating potential of the property. This involves projecting *cash flows* based on rental income and estimating expenses such as property taxes, insurance, maintenance costs, and property management fees. Evaluating the return on investment metrics such as *net operating income (NOI), cap rate, cash-on-cash return,* and *internal rate of return (IRR)* helps determine the profitability of the investment.

2. **Property Condition Assessment:** Assessing the condition of the property is essential to identify any *necessary repairs or renovations.* Conducting inspections helps identify potential issues with the structure, plumbing, electrical systems, and other components. Understanding the scope of required repairs or renovations allows for accurate cost estimation and assessment of the property's overall condition.

3. **Market Analysis:** Analyzing the local market is crucial to evaluate the *supply and demand dynamics, competition,* and *rental market trends.* Assessing the vacancy rates, rental rates, and absorption rates helps gauge the potential rental demand and the market's attractiveness for investment. Additionally, analyzing market trends and future development plans in the

area provides insights into the growth potential and potential risks.

4. **Exit Strategies:** Evaluating exit strategies is important to plan for the future. This involves considering options such as *selling the property*, *refinancing* to access equity, or *optimizing the property* within a portfolio. Understanding the potential exit strategies and their implications on returns helps investors make informed decisions throughout the investment lifecycle.

5. **Financing Considerations:** Assessing financing options and their associated terms is crucial for residential real estate investments. This includes evaluating *mortgage options*, *interest rates*, *loan terms*, and *down payment requirements*. Understanding the financing landscape helps determine the feasibility of the investment and the impact on cash flow and returns.

By evaluating these factors, private equity firms can make informed decisions when assessing residential real estate opportunities. Thorough financial analysis, property condition assessment, market analysis, understanding exit strategies, and considering financing options provide a holistic view of the investment potential. This comprehensive evaluation helps investors identify opportunities, mitigate risks, and optimize their residential real estate investments.

7.5 Risks and Rewards of Investing in Residential Real Estate

In this section, we will explore the risks and rewards of investing in residential real estate. We will discuss the potential rewards, risks, and challenges associated with tenant turnover, rental market volatility, and property maintenance. We will also explore risk mitigation strategies, long-term investment considerations, and provide relevant case studies.

Investing in residential real estate offers both **potential rewards and risks**.

1. On the rewards side, one of the primary benefits is the opportunity to generate **passive income**. By purchasing a property and renting it out, investors can earn a regular stream of rental payments, which can provide a stable and consistent source of income over time.

2. Additionally, residential real estate has the potential for **appreciation**, where the value of the property increases over the long term. This can result in significant gains for investors when they decide to sell the property.

3. Lastly, investing in residential real estate can contribute to **portfolio diversification**. Real estate investments have a low correlation with other asset classes, such as stocks and bonds, which can help reduce overall investment risk.

However, investing in residential real estate also comes with its fair share of **risks and challenges**.

1. One major risk is **tenant turnover**. Finding and retaining reliable tenants can be a challenge, as vacancies can lead to a loss of rental income.

2. Additionally, the rental market can be **volatile**, with fluctuations in demand and rental rates. Investors may face periods of low demand, which can impact their rental income.

3. Moreover, **property maintenance** is another challenge. Property owners are responsible for upkeep and repairs, which can be costly and time-consuming. Failure to adequately maintain the property can lead to a decrease in its value and attractiveness to potential tenants.

To mitigate these risks, several **risk mitigation strategies** can be employed.

1. One key approach is **tenant screening**, which involves conducting thorough background checks on prospective tenants to assess their financial stability and rental history. This can help reduce the likelihood of unreliable tenants and minimize the risk of tenant turnover.
2. Another strategy is employing good **property management** services. Property managers handle day-to-day tasks such as finding tenants, collecting rent, and overseeing property maintenance, which can alleviate the burden on investors.
3. Additionally, having appropriate **insurance coverage**, such as landlord insurance, can provide financial protection in the event of property damage, liability claims, or loss of rental income.

When considering residential real estate as a long-term investment, it's essential to take into account factors such as **property value appreciation** and **market cycles**. Over time, residential properties have historically shown appreciation, which can lead to substantial gains for investors. However, it's important to note that real estate markets are cyclical, with periods of growth and decline. Understanding market cycles and trends can help investors make informed decisions and capitalize on opportunities while mitigating risks. Investing in residential real estate should be approached with a *long-term perspective*, as property values tend to *appreciate over time*, despite short-term fluctuations.

Case studies provide valuable insights into successful and challenging residential real estate investments. These *real-world examples* can highlight various strategies and outcomes.

1. **Successful investments** may showcase properties that have experienced *significant appreciation*, generated *consistent rental income*, and benefited from effective *risk management practices*.
2. On the other hand, **challenging investments** may illustrate situations where properties have faced *prolonged vacancies*, encountered *unexpected maintenance issues*, or suffered from a *decline in property value*. By examining case studies, investors can gain a deeper understanding of the nuances of residential real estate investing and learn from both the triumphs and pitfalls of others.

In conclusion, investing in residential real estate offers potential rewards such as passive income, appreciation, and portfolio diversification. However, it also carries risks and challenges, including tenant turnover, rental market volatility, and property maintenance. These risks can be mitigated through strategies such as tenant screening, property management, and insurance coverage. Long-term investment considerations, such as property value appreciation and market cycles, are crucial for making informed investment decisions. Examining case studies can provide valuable insights into successful and challenging residential real estate investments, offering practical lessons for investors. Overall, investing in residential real estate requires careful consideration, risk management, and a long-term perspective to maximize potential rewards while navigating the associated risks.

Conclusion

In conclusion, investing in private equity residential real estate requires a comprehensive analysis of potential investments and effective risk mitigation strategies. By carefully evaluating properties and considering factors such as location, rental demand, and potential for appreciation, investors can make informed decisions. Furthermore, by actively mitigating risks through tenant screenings, property management, and insurance coverage, investors can protect their investments and increase the likelihood of generating positive returns. Understanding these key concepts and terminologies is essential for individuals looking to invest in residential real estate and maximize their investment potential.

Chapter 8: Investing in Commercial Private Equity Real Estate

Commercial Property - Photo by Abbe Sublett

8.1 What is Commercial Real Estate?

In this section, we will provide a concise overview of commercial real estate. We will define and discuss the key characteristics of commercial real estate, highlighting the distinctions between commercial and residential properties. Furthermore, we will explore the significance of commercial real estate in the economy and its role in private equity investments.

Private equity commercial real estate investing refers to the **investment in commercial properties** by private equity firms or individuals. It involves acquiring, owning, managing, and eventually selling or refinancing commercial properties to generate returns on investment.

Commercial real estate encompasses properties that are **used for business purposes** or **income generation**, such as *office buildings, retail* *centers, industrial warehouses,* and *hotels.* These properties are typically *larger in scale* and have different operational dynamics compared to residential properties.

One key distinction between commercial and residential real estate is the intended use. Commercial properties are primarily utilized for **commercial activities**, such as office spaces for businesses, retail spaces for stores, or warehouses for manufacturing and distribution. In contrast, residential properties are designed for **housing purposes** and typically cater to individuals or families seeking a place to live.

Commercial real estate plays a **crucial role in the economy**. It provides spaces for businesses to operate, creates job opportunities, and contributes to local and national economic growth. Office buildings and retail centers, for example, are essential for economic activities and *consumer spending.* Industrial warehouses are crucial for *manufacturing and logistics,* supporting supply chains and trade. The performance of the commercial real estate sector can serve as an indicator of overall economic health and activity.

Private equity investments in commercial real estate involve acquiring and managing properties with the goal of generating attractive returns. Private equity firms **pool funds from institutional and high-net-worth investors** to invest in commercial properties. These investments often involve active management, such as property improvements, leasing strategies, and operational enhancements, to increase the value of the properties. Private equity investors aim to generate returns through *rental income, property appreciation,* and *eventual sale* or *refinancing* of the properties. Commercial real estate offers the potential for attractive risk-adjusted returns and portfolio diversification for private equity investors.

8.2 Types of Commercial Real Estate Investments

This section explores various commercial real estate investments, including office buildings (single and multi-tenant, Class A and Class B), retail centers (shopping malls, strip malls, standalone retail buildings), industrial properties (warehouses, distribution centers, manufacturing facilities), hospitality properties (hotels, resorts, vacation rentals), and other commercial property types (healthcare facilities, self-storage units, data centers).

Commercial real estate offers a diverse range of investment opportunities across different property types. Here are some common types of commercial real estate investments:

1. **Office Buildings:** Office buildings provide spaces for businesses and professional services. They can be classified based on factors such as *tenant occupancy* (single-tenant or multi-tenant) and *quality* (Class A, Class B, Class C).
   1. *Class A buildings* are typically newer, well-maintained, and located in prime areas, attracting high-quality tenants.
   2. *Class B and Class C buildings* may offer lower rental rates but may require some renovations or have lower occupancy rates.
2. **Retail Centers:** Retail centers include *shopping malls, strip malls,* and *standalone retail buildings.* They house a variety of retail businesses, ranging from national chain stores to local shops.
   1. *Shopping malls* are typically larger and offer a mix of anchor tenants and smaller retailers.
   2. *Strip malls* consist of a row of smaller retail spaces, often anchored by a supermarket or a major retailer.
3. **Industrial Properties:** Industrial properties encompass

warehouses, distribution centers, manufacturing facilities, and *industrial parks.*

1. *Warehouses* serve as storage and distribution spaces for goods and logistics operations.
2. *Distribution centers* are larger facilities that handle the movement of goods on a regional or national scale.
3. *Manufacturing facilities* are designed for production and assembly processes.

4. **Hospitality Properties:** Hospitality properties include *hotels, resorts, vacation rentals,* and *other accommodations.* These properties cater to travelers and tourists, providing lodging, amenities, and services. Investments in hospitality properties are influenced by factors such as location, tourism demand, and the overall health of the hospitality industry.

5. **Other Commercial Property Types:** Commercial real estate investments can extend to other sectors such as *healthcare facilities, self-storage facilities, data centers,* and more.

1. *Healthcare facilities* include hospitals, medical office buildings, and specialized clinics.
2. *Self-storage facilities* provide storage space for individuals and businesses.
3. *Data centers* house servers and computing equipment for data storage and processing.

Each type of commercial property investment carries its own set of considerations, risks, and potential rewards. Factors such as location, market demand, property condition, tenant quality, and economic trends play a significant role in determining the investment potential of a specific property type. It's important for investors to conduct thorough research and due diligence to assess the viability and potential returns of each commercial real estate investment opportunity.

8.3 Key Factors to Consider When Investing in Commercial Real Estate

In this section, we will explore the key factors to consider when investing in commercial real estate. This includes analyzing location, property performance metrics, market trends, and macroeconomic factors. We will also address regulatory and legal considerations.

When investing in commercial real estate, several key factors should be considered to make informed investment decisions. Here are some important factors to consider:

1. **Location Analysis:** The location of a commercial property is a critical factor that can greatly impact its investment potential. Consider factors such as *market demand, accessibility to major transportation routes, proximity to population centers*, and *economic growth* in the area. Analyze demographic trends, population growth, and the overall business climate to assess the potential demand for the property.

2. **Property Performance Metrics:** Evaluate property-specific metrics such as *occupancy rates, lease terms, rental rates*, and *tenant quality*. High occupancy rates indicate strong demand, while long-term lease agreements provide stability and predictable cash flow. Rental rates should be competitive within the market to attract and retain tenants. Assessing the creditworthiness of tenants to ensure consistent rental income.

3. **Market Trends and Outlook:** Understand the supply and demand dynamics of the specific commercial property type

and the local market. Analyze *rental market trends*, *vacancy rates*, and *absorption rates* to gauge market conditions. Consider factors such as new developments, upcoming infrastructure projects, and industry trends that may impact the property's performance.

4. **Macro and Microeconomic Factors:** Evaluate *macroeconomic* indicators such as *interest rates*, *GDP growth*, *employment rates*, and *consumer confidence*. Low interest rates can make financing more affordable, while strong economic growth and employment can contribute to higher tenant demand. Additionally, assess *microeconomic* factors specific to the local market, such as the presence of *major employers*, *industry diversification*, and *economic stability*.

5. **Regulatory and Legal Considerations:** Understand the regulatory and legal landscape governing commercial real estate investments in the specific market. Consider *zoning laws*, *permits*, building codes, and environmental regulations that may impact property development or usage. Research any planned or potential changes in regulations that could affect the property's value or operation.

By considering these factors, investors can assess the potential risks and rewards associated with a commercial real estate investment. Conducting thorough due diligence, market research, and financial analysis can help identify opportunities and mitigate potential risks. It's advisable to work with experienced professionals, such as real estate agents, property managers, and legal advisors, to navigate the complexities of commercial real estate investing successfully.

8.4 How to Evaluate Commercial Real Estate Opportunities

In this section, we will explore evaluating commercial real estate opportunities. This involves financial analysis, risk assessment, due diligence, and exploring different exit strategies.

When evaluating commercial real estate opportunities, it's crucial to conduct a **comprehensive evaluation** that encompasses various aspects of the investment. Here are key factors to consider:

1. **Financial Analysis:** Perform a thorough financial analysis to assess the investment's potential returns. Evaluate cash flow projections, taking into account rental income, operating expenses, and debt service. Calculate key financial metrics such as *capitalization rate (cap rate)*, which compares the property's *net operating income (NOI)* to its purchase price, and *cash-on-cash return*, which measures the annual cash flow relative to the initial investment.

2. **Risk Assessment:** Assess the risks associated with the investment.
   1. Consider *market risk*, including factors like supply and demand dynamics, rental market trends, and economic conditions.
   2. Evaluate *property-specific risks* such as location, condition, tenant mix, and lease terms.
   3. Analyze *tenant risk* by assessing the creditworthiness and stability of existing or prospective tenants.

3. **Due Diligence:** Conduct thorough due diligence to gather information and verify the investment's viability. This may include *property inspections* to assess the physical condition, *title searches* to ensure clear ownership, *environmental assessments* to identify potential risks, and *reviewing lease*

agreements and tenant profiles. Engage professionals such as property inspectors, appraisers, attorneys, and environmental consultants to assist in the due diligence process.

4. **Exit Strategies:** Consider the potential exit strategies for the investment. Determine whether the goal is to *sell the property at a higher price, refinance to leverage equity, recapitalize* by bringing in additional investors, or potentially *take the property public* through an initial public offering (IPO). Understanding potential exit strategies helps shape the investment strategy and aligns with the desired investment horizon.

By considering these factors and conducting thorough evaluations, investors can make informed decisions when assessing commercial real estate opportunities. It's essential to work with experienced professionals, including real estate agents, attorneys, financial advisors, and property managers, to ensure a comprehensive analysis and mitigate potential risks.

8.5 Risks and Rewards of Investing in Commercial Real Estate

In this section, we will explore the risks and rewards of investing in commercial real estate, including income generation, capital appreciation, and portfolio diversification. Mitigating risks through due diligence, risk management, and portfolio diversification is crucial, with long-term considerations including market cycles, cash flow stability, and exit planning. Case studies will provide real-world examples of successful and challenging commercial real estate investments.

Investing in commercial real estate offers both potential rewards and risks. Here are the key factors to consider:

Potential Rewards

1. **Income Generation:** Commercial properties can generate steady rental income, providing a reliable cash flow stream for investors.
2. **Capital Appreciation:** Over time, commercial properties may appreciate in value, allowing investors to benefit from potential capital gains.
3. **Portfolio Diversification:** Commercial real estate can serve as a diversification tool, reducing overall investment risk by adding a different asset class to an investment portfolio.

Risks and Challenges

1. **Market Volatility:** Commercial real estate values can be influenced by market fluctuations, impacting property valuations and investment returns.
2. **Economic Downturns:** Economic recessions or downturns can lead to reduced demand, tenant vacancies, and declining rental rates, affecting cash flow.
3. **Tenant Vacancy:** The risk of tenant vacancies poses potential income disruptions and may require additional expenses for finding new tenants.

Mitigating Risks

1. **Proper Due Diligence:** Thoroughly researching and evaluating properties, markets, and tenants helps investors make informed decisions and mitigate risks.
2. **Risk Management Strategies:** Implementing risk management strategies such as adequate insurance coverage and lease agreements with reliable tenants can minimize potential risks.

3. **Portfolio Diversification:** Spreading investments across different property types, locations, and tenant industries can reduce exposure to specific risks.

Long-Term Investment Considerations

1. **Market Cycles:** Understanding market cycles is crucial for long-term investment success in commercial real estate. Being aware of market dynamics helps in identifying favorable entry and exit points.
2. **Cash Flow Stability:** Assessing the stability and predictability of cash flow is important to ensure the property can generate consistent income over the long term.
3. **Exit Planning:** Having a well-defined exit strategy allows investors to plan for potential liquidity events and maximize returns on their investments.

Case Studies

Analyzing real-life case studies of successful and challenging commercial real estate investments provides *valuable insights* into the factors that contribute to investment success or failure. By studying these cases, investors can learn from past experiences and make more informed investment decisions.

In summary, investing in commercial real estate offers potential rewards such as income generation, capital appreciation, and portfolio diversification. However, it also comes with risks and challenges such as market volatility, economic downturns, and tenant vacancies. Mitigating risks through proper due diligence, risk management strategies, and portfolio diversification is important. Long-term considerations include market cycles, cash flow stability, and exit planning. By studying real-life case studies, investors can gain valuable insights into successful and challenging commercial real estate investments.

Conclusion

Investing in commercial private equity real estate demands expertise, analysis, and meticulous due diligence. It involves diverse property types and aims for returns through rent, appreciation, and exit strategies. Thorough evaluation of location, property performance, markets, economics, and regulations is essential. Diligent inspections, title searches, environmental assessments, and lease reviews form part of the due diligence process. Considering rewards, risks, mitigation strategies, long-term aspects, and real-life case studies contributes to informed decision-making and success in the commercial real estate market.

Chapter 9: Investing in Private Equity Real Estate Office Buildings

Office Building - Photo by kaleb tapp

9.1: Introduction to Office Buildings in Private Equity Real Estate

Office buildings are a significant asset class in the real estate market, and understanding their dynamics is crucial for successful private equity investments.This section provides an overview of office buildings as an asset class and highlights their importance in private equity real estate investments. It discusses market demand and trends in the office space sector, explores the potential benefits and challenges of investing in office buildings, and emphasizes the role of private equity in such investments.

Office buildings are a prominent asset class within private equity real estate investments. These properties are designed to **provide space for businesses** and **professional services**, serving as commercial hubs for various industries. Office buildings play a crucial role in the economy by facilitating business operations, attracting talent, and fostering collaboration among professionals.

Private equity real estate investments in office buildings offer numerous advantages.

1. Firstly, office buildings can generate steady rental income through **long-term lease agreements** with tenants. This provides investors with a reliable cash flow stream and the potential for income growth over time.
2. Additionally, office buildings can **appreciate in value**, offering the potential for capital appreciation upon sale or refinancing.

Market demand and trends play a significant role in office space investments. Factors such as *economic growth*, *urbanization*, *industry expansion*, and *job creation* influence the demand for office spaces. Understanding market dynamics and trends helps investors identify opportunities in thriving markets and gauge the potential for rental rate growth.

Investing in office buildings presents both benefits and challenges.

1. On the positive side, office buildings often attract **high-quality tenants**, including established businesses, professional services firms, and government agencies. These tenants tend to have stable cash flows and can provide long-term occupancy.
2. Furthermore, office buildings offer the potential for **higher rental rates** compared to other commercial real estate sectors.

However, investing in office buildings also comes with challenges.

1. **Market volatility** and **economic downturns** can affect tenant demand and rental rates.
2. Additionally, **changes in technology** and **remote work trends** may impact the demand for office spaces, requiring investors to adapt to evolving market conditions.

Private equity plays a significant role in office building investments. Private equity firms raise capital from institutional and individual investors and **pool these funds** to *acquire*, *develop*, and *manage* office properties.

Private equity investors typically have **extensive expertise** in the commercial real estate sector, allowing them to identify attractive investment opportunities, negotiate favorable terms, and actively manage the properties to enhance value.

In summary, office buildings are an important asset class within private equity real estate investments. They offer steady rental income, potential capital appreciation, and play a crucial role in the economy. Understanding market demand, trends, and the role of private equity is essential for successful office building investments. While there are benefits and challenges associated with investing in office buildings, thorough market analysis, risk assessment, and active property management can help investors navigate the opportunities in this sector.

9.2 Types of Office Buildings

Understanding these various types of office buildings is important for investors and stakeholders in the real estate market. This section provides an overview of the different types of office buildings. It covers classifications such as Class A, Class B, and Class C office buildings, as well as the distinction between single-tenant and multi-tenant office buildings. It also explores the differences between high-rise and low-rise office buildings and highlights the emergence of shared office spaces and co-working environments. Additionally, it mentions specialized office buildings such as medical offices and executive suites.

Office buildings can be classified into different categories based on various factors. Here are the main types of office buildings:

1. **Classifications of Office Buildings:** Office buildings are often categorized into different classes, typically labeled as Class A, Class B, and Class C. These classifications are based on the *quality*, *age*, *location*, *amenities*, and *overall desirability* of the building.
    1. **Class A** buildings are considered *high-quality*, modern, and well-maintained, often located in prime business districts.
    2. **Class B** buildings are typically *older or have slightly lower-quality finishes* but are still functional and attract a range of tenants.
    3. **Class C** buildings are older, may require renovations, and typically offer *lower rental rates* compared to Class A and B properties.
2. **Single-Tenant vs. Multi-Tenant Office Buildings:** Office buildings can be either single-tenant or multi-tenant properties.
    1. **Single-tenant** buildings are occupied by a single tenant, often a large corporation or government entity, and typically have long-term lease agreements.
    2. **Multi-tenant** buildings, on the other hand, accommodate multiple tenants within the same property, offering flexibility and the potential for higher overall rental income.
3. **High-Rise vs. Low-Rise Office Buildings:** Office buildings

can also be categorized based on their height.

1. **High-rise** buildings have numerous floors and offer a *larger total leasable area*. They are commonly found in major urban centers and business districts.
2. **Low-rise** buildings, on the other hand, are typically smaller in scale, with *fewer floors*, and are often found in suburban areas.

4. **Shared Office Spaces and Co-Working Environments:** Shared office spaces and co-working environments have gained popularity in recent years. These spaces provide *flexible workspaces* and amenities that can be rented by individuals or small businesses on a short-term basis. Shared office spaces offer a *cost-effective solution* and foster collaboration and networking opportunities among tenants.

5. **Specialized Office Buildings:** Some office buildings cater to specific industries or purposes. *Medical office buildings*, for example, are designed to accommodate healthcare professionals and medical-related services. *Executive suites* provide fully furnished and equipped offices for businesses that need a professional workspace without the hassle of long-term commitments.

Understanding the different types of office buildings helps investors assess their investment strategies and target specific segments of the market. Factors such as location, tenant demand, lease structures, and market trends should be considered when evaluating opportunities in various types of office buildings.

9.3 Evaluating Office Building Investment Opportunities

This section focuses on evaluating office building investment opportunities. It highlights key factors to consider during the evaluation process. Location analysis, financial analysis, tenant analysis, property condition assessment, and market analysis are crucial for making informed decisions and maximizing the potential of office building investments.

When evaluating office building investment opportunities, several key factors need to be considered:

1. **Location Analysis:** Assessing the location is crucial in evaluating the potential of an office building investment. Factors to consider include *market demand* for office space in the area, *accessibility to transportation* and amenities, and the overall business climate. Understanding the local market dynamics helps determine the level of tenant demand and potential rental rates.

2. **Financial Analysis:** Conducting a thorough financial analysis is essential in assessing the viability of an office building investment. This includes projecting *cash flows*, calculating *net operating income (NOI)*, and analyzing *capitalization rates (cap rates)*. Cash flow projections should consider rental income, operating expenses, and potential vacancy rates. Cap rates help determine the potential return on investment and the building's value relative to its income.

3. **Tenant Analysis:** Analyzing tenants is crucial in evaluating an office building investment. Assessing the *creditworthiness* of existing or potential tenants is important to gauge the stability of rental income. *Lease terms*, such as lease length and rental escalations, also impact cash flow. Examining the *tenant mix* helps assess diversification and potential risks associated with tenant turnover.

4. **Property Condition Assessment:** Evaluating the physical condition of the office building is essential to understand *maintenance needs* and *potential capital expenditures*. Consider factors such as the age of the building, its structural

integrity, and any necessary upgrades or renovations. Assessing the overall condition helps estimate maintenance costs and evaluate the potential for value-add opportunities.

5. **Market Analysis:** Understanding the *supply and demand dynamics* of the office space market is crucial. Analyze *rental rates* in the area, *absorption rates* (the rate at which available space is leased or occupied), and the overall trend in *vacancy rates.* This information helps assess market competitiveness and potential rental income growth.

By conducting a comprehensive evaluation of these factors, investors can assess the potential risks and returns associated with office building investments. This analysis helps inform investment decisions and allows for a more informed and strategic approach to office building investment opportunities.

9.4 Property Management and Tenant Relations

This section focuses on the importance of property management and tenant relations in the context of office building investments. It highlights key aspects such as tenant acquisition and retention strategies, lease negotiations and renewals, tenant improvements and space planning, property maintenance, and facilities management, and monitoring tenant relations and satisfaction. These factors are crucial for maintaining a successful and profitable office building investment by creating a positive tenant experience and maximizing occupancy rates.

Effective property management and tenant relations are essential for successful office building investments. Here are key aspects to consider:

1. **Tenant Acquisition and Retention Strategies:** Developing effective strategies for tenant acquisition and retention is

crucial for maintaining *high occupancy rates*. This involves *marketing the property* to attract quality tenants, *conducting thorough tenant screenings*, and *negotiating lease terms* that are mutually beneficial. Building positive relationships with tenants and addressing their needs and concerns can help increase tenant satisfaction and encourage lease renewals.

2. **Lease Negotiations and Renewals:** Skilled lease negotiations are essential for maximizing rental income and ensuring favorable lease terms. Property managers should *stay informed about market rental rates* and *lease structures*. Proactive lease renewal strategies, such as early engagement with tenants and offering *incentives for renewing leases*, can help minimize vacancy rates and maintain a stable income stream.

3. **Tenant Improvements and Space Planning:** Understanding tenant needs and providing suitable office space solutions is crucial. Tenant improvements, such as *remodeling or customization of office spaces*, can enhance tenant satisfaction and attract high-quality tenants. *Effective space planning*, considering factors like functionality, layout, and flexibility, can optimize the utilization of office space and cater to tenants' specific requirements.

4. **Property Maintenance and Facilities Management:** Maintaining the property's physical condition is essential for tenant satisfaction and asset preservation. Implementing a *proactive maintenance program*, conducting *regular inspections*, and *promptly addressing repair and maintenance issues* are critical. Property managers should ensure *proper upkeep* of common areas, amenities, and building systems to create a conducive and attractive working environment for tenants.

5. **Tenant Relations and Satisfaction Monitoring:** Building

strong relationships with tenants and monitoring their satisfaction levels is key to *tenant retention*. Regular communication, responsiveness to tenant inquiries and concerns, and addressing maintenance requests in a timely manner contribute to positive tenant relations. Implementing *tenant satisfaction surveys* or feedback mechanisms can provide valuable insights and help identify areas for improvement.

By implementing effective property management strategies and fostering positive tenant relations, investors can enhance the value of their office building investments. Satisfied and long-term tenants contribute to stable rental income, reduce vacancy risks, and improve the overall performance of the property. Regularly assessing and addressing tenant needs and maintaining a well-managed property contribute to a positive tenant experience and long-term success in the office building sector.

9.5 Risks and Rewards of Investing in Office Buildings

Understanding the risks and rewards in office building investments is essential for making informed decisions and maximizing investment success. This section focuses on the risks and rewards associated with investing in office buildings. It highlights the potential rewards, risks and challenges, risk mitigation, market factors and case studies of successful and challenging office building investments.

Investing in office buildings can offer a range of potential rewards, but it also comes with certain risks and challenges. Here are the key considerations:

1. **Potential Rewards:** Office buildings can provide a *steady rental income stream* due to long-term lease agreements with

tenants. This offers investors a reliable cash flow. Additionally, office buildings have the potential for *appreciation* in value over time, allowing investors to benefit from capital appreciation upon sale or refinancing. *Value-add opportunities*, such as property renovations or repositioning, can further enhance the property's value and generate higher returns.

2. **Risks and Challenges:** *Economic downturns* can impact the demand for office space and increase vacancy rates. *Market conditions*, including changes in supply and demand dynamics, can affect rental rates and occupancy levels. *Tenant defaults* or *ternant bankruptcies* can also pose risks, leading to periods of vacancy and potential loss of rental income.

3. **Risk Mitigation:** *Diversification across multiple office buildings* or geographic locations can help reduce risk. Having a mix of tenants and lease structures, such as *staggered lease expirations* or *long-term leases*, can mitigate the impact of tenant defaults. *Effective property management*, including proactive maintenance, tenant relations, and addressing tenant needs promptly, can help minimize vacancy rates and enhance tenant satisfaction.

4. **Market Factors Impacting Investments:** *Technological advancements* and *remote work trends* have the potential to impact office building investments. The rise of remote work and flexible work arrangements may influence tenant demand and require investors to adapt to *changing market dynamics*. Understanding these trends and their potential impact on the office space sector is crucial for making informed investment decisions.

5. **Case Studies:** Examining real-life case studies of successful and challenging office building investments provides *valuable insights*. Successful case studies can highlight strategies that

led to high occupancy rates, rental income growth, and value appreciation. Challenging case studies offer lessons learned from factors such as economic downturns, tenant defaults, or poor property management.

Understanding the risks and rewards associated with investing in office buildings helps investors make informed decisions. Mitigating risks through diversification, lease structures, and effective property management is essential for long-term success. Monitoring market factors and adapting to changing trends ensures investors stay ahead in the evolving office space sector. By analyzing case studies, investors can learn from past experiences and apply best practices to their own office building investments.

Conclusion

In conclusion, investing in private equity real estate office buildings necessitates a comprehensive understanding of the concepts and terminologies involved. Thorough analysis, including location analysis, financial analysis, tenant analysis, property condition assessment, and market analysis, helps identify opportunities and mitigate risks. Additionally, effective property management and strong tenant relations are vital for maximizing returns and ensuring the long-term success of office building investments.

Chapter 10: Investing in Private Equity Real Estate Retail Buildings

10.1 Introduction to Retail Buildings in Private Equity Real Estate

Understanding the dynamics of retail buildings is crucial for investors looking to navigate the retail sector and maximize their returns in private equity real estate. This section provides an introduction to retail buildings as an asset class in private equity real estate. It emphasizes the importance of retail buildings in private equity investments and highlights market trends and dynamics in the retail sector. Additionally, it discusses the potential benefits and challenges associated with investing in retail buildings.

Retail buildings play a significant role in private equity real estate investments. They are an essential asset class that offers unique opportunities and challenges. Understanding the basics of retail buildings in private equity real estate is crucial for investors.

Retail buildings refer to properties that are specifically designed and used for commercial activities, such as *retail stores, shopping malls, strip malls,* and *standalone retail buildings.* These buildings serve as spaces where *businesses interact* with customers and sell products or services.

Retail buildings hold importance in private equity real estate investments for several reasons.

1. Firstly, they offer the potential for *stable cash flow* through **long-term leases** with tenants. Retail tenants typically sign leases with extended durations, providing investors with consistent rental income.
2. Secondly, retail buildings can offer the opportunity for **value appreciation** over time. Prime retail locations and successful retail centers can experience increased property values, allowing investors to benefit from capital appreciation.
3. Lastly, retail buildings contribute to **portfolio diversification** by adding a different asset class to an investment portfolio, alongside other real estate sectors like residential, office, and industrial.

Market trends and dynamics play a crucial role in the performance of retail buildings. Factors such as *consumer spending habits, economic conditions,* and *shifts in retail models* (e.g., e-commerce) can impact the demand for retail space. Understanding these trends and adapting to changes is essential for investors to make informed investment decisions.

Investing in retail buildings also comes with its own set of benefits and challenges. One benefit is the potential for **higher rental rates** compared to other real estate sectors. Well-located retail properties in high-demand areas can attract popular retailers, leading to higher rents.

However, retail buildings face challenges such as **changing consumer preferences**, competition from e-commerce, and market volatility. These factors can impact tenant occupancy and rental rates, requiring investors to stay adaptable and proactive in their investment strategies.

Private equity plays a significant role in retail building investments. **Private equity firms** and funds often invest in retail properties to generate attractive returns for their investors. They bring *expertise*, *capital*, and *value-added* strategies to enhance the performance of retail buildings. Private equity investors typically focus on value creation through *active management*, including *leasing strategies*, *property improvements*, and *repositioning* initiatives.

In summary, retail buildings hold a prominent place in private equity real estate investments. Understanding their role, market trends, and potential benefits and challenges is essential for investors seeking to capitalize on opportunities in this asset class. The involvement of private equity further contributes to the growth and optimization of retail building investments.

10.2 Types of Retail Buildings

Understanding the various types of retail buildings is essential for investors looking to diversify their portfolios and capitalize on different market opportunities within the retail sector. This section explores the different types of retail buildings in private equity real estate. It includes shopping malls, such as regional malls, neighborhood malls, and outlet malls. It also covers strip centers and retail plazas, standalone retail buildings, lifestyle centers, mixed-use developments, retail condominiums, and retail park investments.

When it comes to retail buildings in private equity real estate, there are several types that investors can consider. Each type offers unique characteristics and investment opportunities. Here are some common types of retail buildings:

1. **Shopping Malls:** Shopping malls are large-scale retail complexes that house multiple stores, often *anchored by department stores* or major retailers. Shopping malls typically offer a wide range of amenities and entertainment options to attract shoppers. There are various types of shopping malls, including:
     1. *regional malls*, which serve a wide geographic area and offer a diverse range of stores;
     2. *neighborhood malls*, which cater to local communities with convenience-focused retailers; and
     3. *outlet malls*, which feature discounted brand-name merchandise.
2. **Strip Centers and Retail Plazas:** Strip centers, also known as strip malls or retail plazas, consist of a *row of attached or detached retail units*. They are typically located along busy commercial corridors and offer convenience-oriented retail options. Strip centers often have a mix of retailers, including *grocery stores*, *restaurants*, and *service-oriented businesses*. These retail buildings are popular due to their accessibility and affordability.
3. **Standalone Retail Buildings:** Standalone retail buildings refer to single retail properties that are not part of a larger complex. They can range from *small freestanding stores* to *large big-box retail locations*. Standalone buildings offer flexibility in terms of tenant customization and can be designed to suit specific retail concepts or brands.
4. **Lifestyle Centers and Mixed-Use Developments:** Lifestyle centers are retail destinations that *combine shopping with*

leisure and entertainment experiences. They often feature outdoor spaces, upscale retailers, restaurants, and entertainment venues. *Mixed-use developments* integrate retail spaces with other components such as *residential, office*, and *recreational areas*, creating a vibrant live-work-play environment. These types of retail buildings cater to consumers seeking a more experiential and integrated shopping experience.

5. **Retail Condominiums and Retail Park Investments:** Retail condominiums involve the ownership of individual units within a larger retail complex. Investors can purchase and own *specific retail spaces within the building*. Retail parks are typically characterized by a cluster of standalone retail buildings with shared parking areas. These parks often have a mix of large-format retailers and are located in suburban areas.

Each type of retail building presents its own set of opportunities and considerations. Factors such as location, tenant mix, market demand, and local demographics should be carefully evaluated when assessing investment opportunities in these retail building types. Understanding the unique characteristics and dynamics of each type is crucial for private equity real estate investors seeking to enter the retail sector.

10.3 Evaluating Retail Building Investment Opportunities

This section focuses on evaluating retail building investment opportunities and covers key factors to consider during the evaluation process. Location analysis, financial analysis, tenant analysis, property condition, and market analysis are crucial for making informed decisions and maximizing the potential of retail building investments.

Evaluating retail building investment opportunities requires a comprehensive analysis of various factors. Here are key considerations when assessing potential investments:

1. **Location Analysis:** Understanding the market demand and suitability of the location is critical. Factors to consider include the population density, *demographics*, and *consumer profile* in the area. Analyzing the surrounding competition and proximity to residential areas, office complexes, and transportation hubs helps assess the potential foot traffic and customer base for the retail building.

2. **Financial Analysis:** Conducting a thorough financial analysis is essential to evaluate the potential returns and profitability of the investment. Cash flow projections should account for *rental income, operating expenses*, and potential *vacancies*. Calculating the *net operating income (NOI)* and assessing the *capitalization rate (cap rate)* allows investors to compare the investment's performance against market benchmarks.

3. **Tenant Analysis:** Evaluating the tenant mix within the retail building is crucial. Assessing the *types of retailers* and their suitability for the location and target customer base is important. *Lease terms*, including duration, rental escalations, and tenant responsibilities, should be carefully reviewed. Analyzing the *creditworthiness and financial stability of tenants* helps gauge the risk of tenant defaults and the overall stability of the rental income.

4. **Property Condition Assessment:** Evaluating the physical condition of the retail building is vital. Assessing the *age, structural integrity*, and *maintenance needs* of the property is necessary to estimate potential renovation or improvement costs. Identifying any *compliance issues*, such as zoning

regulations or building codes, is also important.

5. **Market Analysis:** Understanding retail *market trends* and the *performance of existing tenants* in the area provides valuable insights. Analyzing historical and current rental rates, vacancy rates, and absorption rates helps gauge the market dynamics. Assessing foot traffic and customer patterns in the vicinity of the retail building provides insight into potential customer demand.

By conducting a comprehensive analysis that includes location analysis, financial analysis, tenant analysis, property condition assessment, and market analysis, investors can make informed decisions about retail building investments. This evaluation process helps identify opportunities, assess risks, and determine the viability and potential profitability of the investment. Thorough due diligence is crucial to mitigate risks and maximize returns in the retail sector.

10.4 Property Management and Tenant Relations

This section highlights the importance of property management and tenant relations in retail building investments. It covers tenant acquisition and retention strategies, lease negotiations and rent roll analysis, tenant mix and space planning, effective marketing and promotions, and property maintenance and facilities management. Successful property management and tenant relations are key to maximizing the value and profitability of retail building investments.

Effective property management and tenant relations are essential for successful retail building investments. Here are key areas to focus on:

1. **Tenant Acquisition and Retention Strategies:** Developing effective strategies to attract and retain quality tenants is crucial for the long-term success of a retail building. This

includes actively seeking out reputable retailers that *align with the target market* and have a *track record of success.* Offering attractive lease terms, such as competitive rental rates and flexible lease structures, can help attract desirable tenants. Additionally, maintaining *positive relationships with existing tenants, addressing their concerns promptly,* and *providing exceptional customer service* can contribute to tenant satisfaction and retention.

2. **Lease Negotiations and Rent Roll Analysis:** Skilled lease negotiations are vital to secure favorable terms and maximize rental income. Analyzing the rent roll, which outlines the lease agreements and rental income generated by each tenant, helps identify lease expirations, rental escalations, and potential vacancies. Understanding *market rental rates* and conducting *market comparisons* enables landlords to negotiate competitive lease terms while ensuring the profitability of the investment.

3. **Tenant Mix and Space Planning:** Careful consideration of the tenant mix within the retail building is crucial. Striving for a complementary mix of tenants that cater to different consumer needs and preferences helps create a vibrant and attractive retail environment. Understanding the target market and tenant synergies can aid in strategic space planning to optimize tenant visibility and foot traffic flow. This includes determining optimal store layouts, signage placement, and common area design to enhance the overall shopping experience.

4. **Marketing and Promotions for Retail Tenants:** Supporting and promoting retail tenants can drive foot traffic and increase sales within the retail building. Collaborating with tenants to *develop marketing strategies, coordinating events,* and implementing effective *promotional campaigns* can

enhance tenant visibility and attract customers. Utilizing various marketing channels, such as *social media*, *digital advertising*, and *local partnerships*, helps create awareness and generate consumer interest in the retail offerings.

5. **Property Maintenance and Facilities Management:** Maintaining the physical condition of the retail building and providing efficient facilities management services are essential for tenant satisfaction and operational efficiency. *Regular inspections*, *timely repairs*, and *proactive maintenance* help ensure the safety, functionality, and aesthetics of the property. Additionally, effective facilities management, including waste management, security services, and parking management, contributes to a positive tenant experience and a well-maintained retail environment.

By focusing on tenant acquisition and retention strategies, lease negotiations, tenant mix, marketing efforts, and property maintenance, investors can enhance the overall performance and value of retail building investments. A strong property management approach ensures tenant satisfaction, maximizes rental income, and creates a vibrant retail environment that attracts customers and supports the long-term success of the investment.

10.5 Risks and Rewards of Investing in Retail Buildings

Understanding the risks and rewards in retail building investments is crucial for making informed decisions and achieving success in the dynamic retail market. This section focuses on the risks and rewards associated with investing in retail buildings. It highlights the potential rewards, risks and challenges, risk mitigation strategies, market factors impacting retail building investments, and case studies of successful and challenging retail building investments.

Investing in retail buildings offers both potential rewards and inherent risks. Understanding these factors is crucial for making informed investment decisions. Here are the key considerations:

1. **Potential Rewards:**
   - *Rental Income:* Retail buildings can generate steady rental income from tenants, providing a consistent cash flow stream for investors.
   - *Value Appreciation:* Well-located and well-managed retail properties have the potential for capital appreciation over time.
   - *Tenant Stability:* Establishing long-term relationships with stable and reputable tenants can contribute to consistent occupancy rates and rental income.

2. **Risks and Challenges:**
   - *Market Shifts:* The retail industry is subject to market shifts and evolving consumer preferences. Changes in shopping habits and the rise of e-commerce can impact the performance of retail buildings.
   - *Changing Consumer Behavior:* Shifts in consumer preferences and spending patterns can affect tenant demand and the viability of certain retail concepts.
   - *Tenant Turnover:* High tenant turnover can lead to increased vacancies and disrupt cash flow, requiring additional efforts to attract new tenants.

3. **Risk Mitigation:**
   - *Diversification:* Spreading investments across different retail buildings and locations can help mitigate the risk of relying on a single property or

tenant.

- *Lease Structures:* Implementing lease structures that include minimum lease terms, rental escalations, and tenant responsibilities can provide stability and predictability.
- *Tenant Quality Analysis:* Conducting thorough tenant quality analysis, including assessing the financial stability and track record of potential tenants, can help minimize the risk of tenant defaults.

4. **Market Factors Impacting Retail Building Investments:**
   - *E-commerce:* The rise of e-commerce has transformed the retail landscape, affecting brick-and-mortar stores. Investors need to consider the impact of online shopping and how it may shape tenant demand and the competitive environment.
   - *Economic Conditions:* Economic conditions, such as GDP growth, employment rates, and consumer confidence, can influence consumer spending and overall retail performance. Understanding the broader economic climate is crucial for assessing the viability of retail building investments.

5. **Case Studies:** Examining real-life examples of successful and challenging retail building investments can provide valuable insights into industry trends, best practices, and potential pitfalls. These case studies can help investors learn from past experiences and make more informed investment decisions.

By understanding the potential rewards, risks, and challenges of investing in retail buildings, and implementing risk mitigation strategies, investors can navigate the dynamic retail market and optimize their investment outcomes. Monitoring market trends, consumer behavior, and economic conditions is essential for staying informed and adapting investment strategies accordingly.

Conclusion

In conclusion, investing in private equity real estate retail buildings requires a comprehensive analysis and a focus on tenant relations. Retail buildings, including shopping malls, strip centers, standalone buildings, and lifestyle centers, are a significant asset class within private equity real estate. Thorough analyses help assess risks and rewards. Effective tenant relations are crucial for stability and profitability. Attention to tenant mix, space planning, marketing, and property maintenance enhances tenant satisfaction. By considering these factors, investors can make informed decisions, mitigate risks, and maximize returns in the private equity real estate retail building sector.

Chapter 11: Investing in Private Equity Real Estate Industrial Buildings

Warehouse - Photo by Ruchindra Gunasekara

11.1 Introduction to Industrial Buildings in Private Equity Real Estate

This section provides an overview of industrial buildings in private equity real estate investments. Industrial buildings are crucial for manufacturing, warehousing, logistics, and distribution operations. They offer potential benefits like stable rental income and value appreciation. However, challenges such as customization requirements, tenant turnover risks, and economic fluctuations exist. Private equity provides capital and expertise for successful investments. Understanding the unique characteristics and market dynamics of industrial buildings is essential for investors in private equity real estate.

Industrial buildings play a significant role in private equity real estate investments. Here's an introduction to industrial buildings in the context of private equity:

1. **Overview of Industrial Buildings as an Asset Class:** Industrial buildings encompass a wide range of properties, including *warehouses, distribution centers, manufacturing facilities*, and *logistics hubs*. These buildings are designed to support industrial activities, storage, and the movement of goods. They often feature large floor areas, high ceilings, loading docks, and specialized infrastructure.

2. **Importance of Industrial Buildings in Private Equity Real Estate Investments:** Industrial buildings are essential in private equity real estate portfolios due to their *income-generating potential* and *capital appreciation*. They serve as crucial components of the supply chain, supporting the logistics and distribution needs of various industries. The *growing e-commerce sector* and increased demand for efficient storage and distribution facilities further underscore the importance of industrial buildings in private equity investments.

3. **Market Demand and Growth Potential in the Industrial Sector:** The industrial sector has experienced robust demand and growth in recent years. Factors such as the *rise of e-commerce, globalization of supply chains*, and *evolving consumer preferences* have fueled the need for modern and strategically located industrial buildings. This has led to increased investor interest in this asset class, driven by the potential for long-term income stability and capital appreciation.

4. **Potential Benefits and Challenges of Investing in Industrial Buildings:** Investing in industrial buildings offers

several benefits, including *stable rental income, long-term lease agreements,* and *tenant demand* driven by the industrial sector's growth. Industrial properties often have *lower tenant turnover* compared to other asset classes. However, challenges such as changes in technology, evolving tenant requirements, and *location-dependent market dynamics* should be considered.

5. **Role of Private Equity in Industrial Building Investments:** Private equity plays a crucial role in industrial building investments by providing capital, expertise, and strategic guidance. Private equity firms can identify *value-add opportunities, reposition underperforming assets,* and *leverage their networks* to attract high-quality tenants and achieve operational efficiencies. They also contribute to the development and redevelopment of industrial properties to meet the evolving needs of tenants and the market.

Industrial buildings offer unique advantages and investment opportunities within the private equity real estate space. Understanding the dynamics of the industrial sector, market demand, and the role of private equity helps investors make informed decisions and capitalize on the potential benefits of industrial building investments.

11.2 Types of Industrial Buildings

Industrial buildings encompass various types that serve different purposes. SOme industrial buildings include warehouses distribution centers and logistics facilities, manufacturing plants and industrial complexes, flex space and business parks, cold storage facilities and refrigerated warehouses, and data centers and research & development facilities. Understanding the different types of industrial buildings allows investors to target specific sectors and tailor their investments to meet the demands of various industries.

Industrial buildings encompass various types that cater to different industrial activities. Here are the key types of industrial buildings:

1. **Warehouses:** Warehouses are dedicated to the *storage, handling,* and *distribution of goods.* They can range from large-scale distribution centers serving regional or national markets to smaller logistics facilities supporting local businesses. Warehouses typically feature expansive floor areas, high ceilings, loading docks, and sometimes automated systems for efficient material handling.

2. **Manufacturing Plants and Industrial Complexes:** These buildings are designed for *production and manufacturing activities.* They house machinery, assembly lines, and specialized infrastructure required for manufacturing processes. Industrial complexes often consist of multiple interconnected buildings that support various stages of production, including raw material storage, production lines, and finished goods warehousing.

3. **Flex Space and Business Parks:** Flex space refers to *flexible industrial buildings* that can be adapted for multiple uses. They offer a combination of office space and warehouse/storage areas, providing flexibility for tenants with diverse operational needs. Business parks are developments that incorporate a mix of flex space, office space, and sometimes retail facilities, creating a cohesive and business-friendly environment.

4. **Cold Storage Facilities and Refrigerated Warehouses:** These specialized industrial buildings are equipped with *temperature-controlled environments* to accommodate perishable goods, pharmaceuticals, or other temperature-

sensitive products. Cold storage facilities and refrigerated warehouses require specific infrastructure, such as refrigeration systems and insulated storage areas, to maintain the desired temperature conditions.

5. **Specialized Industrial Buildings:** In addition to the above types, there are specialized industrial buildings tailored to specific industries or activities. Examples include *data centers* that house computer systems and IT infrastructure, *research and development facilities* that support scientific research and innovation, and *specialized manufacturing facilities* designed for specific industries such as automotive or aerospace.

These different types of industrial buildings cater to a range of industrial activities and play critical roles in supporting supply chains, manufacturing processes, and storage needs. Understanding the specific requirements and market dynamics associated with each type is crucial when evaluating industrial building investment opportunities in private equity real estate.

11.3 Evaluating Industrial Building Investment Opportunities

When evaluating investment opportunities in industrial buildings, it is important to conduct a comprehensive analysis including *location analysis*, *financial analysis*, *tenant analysis*, *property condition assessment*, and *market analysis*. By considering these factors, investors can make informed decisions and maximize the potential of their industrial building investments.

Location analysis plays a crucial role in evaluating industrial building investments. *Proximity to transportation hubs* and *supply chains* is of utmost importance. A strategically located property with easy access to major highways, ports, and airports can significantly enhance the efficiency of logistics operations. Additionally, being close to suppliers and customers can reduce transportation costs and improve overall supply chain management.

Financial analysis is another critical aspect of evaluating industrial building investments.

1. *Cash flow projections* are essential for understanding the potential returns on investment. This analysis involves estimating the income and expenses associated with the property, including rent, operating costs, and property management fees.
2. *Net Operating Income (NOI)* is a key metric that helps determine the property's profitability.
3. Investors should also consider the *capitalization rate (cap rate)*, which is the ratio between the property's net operating income and its market value. A lower cap rate indicates *higher demand* and *potentially higher returns*.

Tenant analysis is crucial to assess the stability and desirability of potential tenants.

1. *Lease terms*, such as the duration and rental escalations, can significantly impact the property's cash flow and long-term profitability.
2. Evaluating the *creditworthiness* and financial stability of tenants is essential to mitigate the risk of default and vacancy.
3. Furthermore, analyzing *industry demand* and *trends* can provide insights into the potential growth or decline of specific sectors, helping investors identify the most promising tenant prospects.

A thorough **property condition assessment** is vital to understanding the physical characteristics and suitability of the industrial building. Key factors to consider include the building's *size*, clear *height (vertical distance from the floor to the ceiling)*, and the *number and functionality of loading docks*. These aspects can directly affect the property's versatility and its ability to accommodate various types of industrial activities. Additionally, assessing the overall *structural integrity*, *maintenance history*, and *potential renovation or repair requirements* is crucial for estimating future expenses and determining the property's value.

Lastly, conducting a comprehensive **market analysis** is essential to evaluate industrial building investment opportunities.

1. Understanding industrial market trends, such as *supply and demand* dynamics, can help investors identify emerging or declining markets.
2. *Absorption rates*, which measure the pace at which available space is leased or sold, provide valuable insights into the market's activity level and potential competition.
3. *Rental rates* in the area should be assessed to ensure the property's potential for competitive leasing income.
4. Market analysis also involves evaluating *local regulations*, *zoning restrictions*, and any planned or ongoing *infrastructure developments* that may impact the industrial property's value and marketability.

In conclusion, evaluating industrial building investment opportunities requires a multifaceted approach. Location analysis, financial analysis, tenant analysis, property condition assessment, and market analysis are all essential components of a comprehensive evaluation. By considering these factors in detail, investors can make informed decisions and maximize their chances of success in the industrial real estate market.

11.4 Property Management and Tenant Relations

Effective property management and positive tenant relations are crucial for the success of industrial building investments. Property managers need to implement strategies for tenant acquisition and retention, handle lease negotiations and renewals, oversee tenant improvements and build-to-suit considerations, ensure proper property maintenance and facility management, and ensure compliance with industrial building standards and regulations.

Tenant acquisition and retention strategies are essential for maintaining a high occupancy rate and minimizing vacancies. Property managers should actively *market the available spaces, target potential tenants* within relevant industries, and showcase the property's *unique selling points*. Additionally, developing *strong relationships* with existing tenants and providing *excellent customer service* can contribute to tenant satisfaction and increase the likelihood of lease renewals.

Lease negotiations and renewals require careful attention to detail. Property managers should be well-versed in *lease terms and conditions, rent escalations*, and *legal requirements*. They should engage in proactive communication with tenants to address any concerns and negotiate *favorable lease terms* that benefit both parties. A thorough understanding of market conditions and rental rates is crucial during lease negotiations to ensure competitive and fair agreements.

Tenant improvements and build-to-suit considerations involve customizing the space to meet specific tenant requirements. Property managers need to collaborate with tenants and contractors to plan and execute the necessary modifications or construction. This process includes *obtaining necessary permits, coordinating construction timelines*, and *ensuring compliance* with building codes and regulations. Effective management of tenant improvements can enhance tenant satisfaction and attract high-quality tenants.

Property maintenance and facility management are essential to preserve the value and functionality of industrial buildings. Property managers should establish regular maintenance schedules, conduct inspections, and promptly address any repairs or maintenance issues. They need to ensure that the property's infrastructure, including HVAC systems, electrical systems, and plumbing, is in good working condition. Additionally, implementing energy-efficient practices and sustainable initiatives can benefit both tenants and the environment.

Compliance with industrial building standards and regulations is of utmost importance. Property managers must stay up-to-date with *relevant codes*, *permits*, and *safety regulations* to ensure that the property meets all legal requirements. This includes *fire safety measures*, *accessibility standards*, *environmental regulations*, and *occupational health and safety guidelines*. Regular inspections and audits should be conducted to identify and rectify any compliance issues.

In summary, effective property management and tenant relations require a comprehensive approach. Tenant acquisition and retention strategies, lease negotiations and renewals, tenant improvements and build-to-suit considerations, property maintenance and facility management, and compliance with industrial building standards and regulations are all vital aspects of successful property management. By prioritizing these areas and maintaining positive tenant relationships, property managers can enhance the value and profitability of industrial building investments.

11.5 Risks and Rewards of Investing in Industrial Buildings

Investing in industrial buildings offers both potential rewards and risks that need to be carefully evaluated. In this section we look at the potential rewards, risks and challenges, risk mitigation techniques, market factors and case studies of industrial investing. By understanding these factors investors can make informed decisions and navigate the risks and rewards associated with investing in industrial buildings.

Investing in industrial buildings offers potential rewards, but also comes with risks and challenges that investors should carefully consider.

Some of the **potential rewards** include rental income, long-term lease stability, and portfolio diversification.

1. *Rental income* from industrial buildings can provide a steady *cash flow* for investors. Industrial properties are often in *high demand* due to the need for warehousing, manufacturing, and logistics facilities. Well-located and well-managed industrial buildings can attract reliable tenants and generate consistent rental income.
2. *Long-term lease stability* is another benefit of investing in industrial buildings. Many industrial tenants prefer longer lease terms to establish *operational stability* and *avoid frequent relocations*. This can provide investors with a predictable income stream and minimize the risk of frequent tenant turnover.
3. Industrial buildings also offer an opportunity for *portfolio diversification*. Including industrial properties in an investment portfolio can help *spread risk* and *reduce reliance on a single asset class*. Diversification can provide a buffer against market fluctuations and contribute to overall portfolio stability.

However, investing in industrial buildings also entails **risks and challenges**.

1. *Economic downturns* can negatively impact industrial real estate, as businesses may downsize or experience financial difficulties, leading to *higher vacancy rates*. Investors should be prepared for potential fluctuations in rental income during economic downturns.

2. *Tenant turnover* is another risk factor. Industrial tenants *may relocate due to business needs, changing market conditions*, or *lease expirations*. Vacancies can result in income loss and additional costs associated with finding new tenants. Investors should carefully evaluate tenant stability and industry demand to mitigate this risk.

3. *Market oversupply* is a challenge that can affect industrial building investments. If there is an excessive supply of industrial properties in a specific market, it can lead to *increased competition, lower rental rates*, and *longer periods of vacancy*. Thorough market analysis is crucial to identify potential oversupply risks and select markets with favorable supply-demand dynamics.

To **mitigate risks**, investors can employ various strategies.

1. *Diversification* across different geographical areas and property types can help spread risk.

2. Implementing *lease structures* that include rent escalations and longer lease terms can provide stability and income growth.

3. Regular *property maintenance* and proactive tenant relationship management can contribute to tenant satisfaction and reduce turnover.

Market factors can significantly impact industrial building investments.

1. The rise of *e-commerce* has increased demand for industrial properties to support warehousing and distribution operations.
2. Additionally, *shifts in supply chain dynamics*, such as the relocation of manufacturing facilities or changes in global trade policies, can influence the demand for industrial space. Investors should closely monitor these market factors to make informed investment decisions.

Case studies of successful and challenging industrial building investments can provide *valuable insights*. Examples of successful investments can highlight factors such as *strategic location*, *strong tenant relationships*, and *effective property management*. Challenging cases can *shed light on risks*, such as market fluctuations or tenant-related issues, and the importance of risk mitigation strategies.

In conclusion, investing in industrial buildings offers potential rewards in the form of rental income, long-term lease stability, and portfolio diversification. However, investors should be aware of the risks and challenges, including economic downturns, tenant turnover, and market oversupply. Mitigating risks through diversification, lease structures, and property maintenance is crucial. Monitoring market factors and learning from case studies can help investors make informed decisions and maximize the potential rewards of investing in industrial buildings.

Conclusion

In conclusion, investing in private equity real estate industrial buildings requires a comprehensive understanding of the key concepts and terminologies discussed. Thorough analysis of location, financials, tenants, property condition, and market trends is crucial for making informed investment decisions. Furthermore, maintaining positive tenant relations and implementing effective property management strategies contribute to the success and long-term stability of industrial building investments.

Chapter 12: Investing in Private Equity Real Estate Hospitality Buildings

Hotel - Photo by Francesca Saraco

12.1 Introduction to Hospitality Buildings in Private Equity Real Estate

Hospitality buildings, including *hotels*, *resorts*, and other accommodation establishments, are an important asset class in private equity real estate investments. These properties cater to the growing demand for travel and accommodation, making them an attractive investment opportunity.

Hospitality buildings offer unique characteristics that set them apart from other real estate asset classes. They provide a combination of *real estate and operating business components*, creating potential for both property appreciation and revenue generation. Investors can benefit from various income streams, including room revenues, food and beverage sales, and event hosting.

The **importance of hospitality buildings in private equity real estate investments** is evident in the industry's size and growth potential. The global hospitality sector has experienced substantial growth over the years, driven by increasing international travel, rising disposable incomes, and changing consumer preferences. This growth presents opportunities for investors to capitalize on the demand for accommodation and related services.

Market demand and trends play a significant role in the attractiveness of hospitality buildings as investments. Factors such as tourism trends, business travel patterns, and emerging markets influence the demand for accommodation. It is essential for investors to **stay informed about market dynamics**, including supply and demand imbalances, competitive landscape, and emerging hospitality concepts and technologies.

Investing in hospitality buildings offers potential benefits, but it also comes with unique challenges.

1. **Benefits** include potential for *attractive returns, diversification* within a real estate portfolio, and the ability to *leverage the operational expertise* of hospitality management companies.
2. However, **challenges** may arise from factors such as *seasonality, economic fluctuations, regulatory constraints*, and *intense competition* within the hospitality sector.

Private equity plays a significant role in hospitality building investments by *providing capital and expertise*. Private equity firms often seek opportunities to acquire and enhance hospitality properties, aiming to *improve operational efficiency, enhance guest experiences*, and *maximize returns*. Their involvement can lead to value creation through strategic repositioning, renovations, and rebranding efforts.

In conclusion, hospitality buildings are a prominent asset class in private equity real estate investments. They offer a unique blend of real estate and operating business components, presenting opportunities for revenue generation and property appreciation. Understanding market demand and trends, as well as the benefits and challenges associated with hospitality building investments, is crucial for successful investment decisions. Private equity firms play a vital role in capitalizing on these opportunities and adding value to hospitality properties.

12.2 Types of Hospitality Buildings

Hospitality buildings encompass various types of accommodations that cater to different traveler preferences and budgets. Understanding these different types is essential for private equity investors considering hospitality building investments. Some common types include *hotels* (full-service, limited-service, boutique), *resorts* and *vacation properties*, *extended stay accommodations*, *bed and breakfasts*, and *hostels and budget accommodations*.

Hotels are the most familiar type of hospitality building. They range from *full-service hotels*, which offer a wide range of amenities and services such as restaurants, room service, and conference facilities, to limited-service hotels, which provide basic accommodations without extensive amenities. *Boutique hotels* are characterized by their unique designs, intimate atmosphere, and personalized service, often appealing to niche markets or specific themes.

Resorts and vacation properties cater to leisure travelers seeking a comprehensive vacation experience. These properties often include amenities such as *pools, spas, recreational facilities*, and *entertainment options*. Resorts can be located in various settings, including beachfront, mountainous, or urban areas, offering diverse experiences to guests.

Extended stay accommodations are designed for guests who require longer-term stays. These properties typically provide *spacious rooms or suites with kitchenettes* or fully equipped kitchens. They cater to business travelers, families, or individuals in need of *temporary housing,* offering the convenience and comfort of a home-like environment.

Bed and breakfasts (B&Bs) offer a more intimate and personalized lodging experience. These establishments are usually *small-scale,* owner-operated properties that provide overnight accommodations and include breakfast as part of the stay. B&Bs often have a cozy atmosphere, unique décor, and a focus on hospitality and personalized service.

Hostels and budget accommodations target budget-conscious travelers, including backpackers, students, and solo travelers. These properties provide *affordable shared or private rooms*, often with communal areas and shared facilities such as kitchens, bathrooms, and lounges. Hostels foster a social atmosphere, encouraging interaction among guests.

Each type of hospitality building presents its own investment opportunities and considerations. Understanding the preferences and demands of target guests is crucial for selecting the right property type and ensuring its market viability and profitability.

12.3 Evaluating Hospitality Building Investment Opportunities

Evaluating hospitality building investment opportunities requires a comprehensive analysis of various factors. Key considerations include *location analysis, financial analysis, brand analysis*, property condition assessment, and *market analysis.*

Location analysis is crucial in determining the potential success of a hospitality investment. It involves assessing *tourism demand* in the area, *proximity to popular attractions* or business centers, and accessibility to transportation hubs. Understanding the local market and its potential for growth is essential for selecting a location that can attract a steady stream of guests.

Financial analysis focuses on the revenue generation potential of the hospitality building. Key metrics to consider include *occupancy rates, average daily rate (ADR)*, and *revenue per available room (RevPAR)*. These metrics provide insights into the property's *revenue performance, pricing strategies*, and *market competitiveness*. It is important to assess the property's historical financial performance and project future cash flows.

Brand analysis is relevant for properties affiliated with established hotel brands. Evaluating the *brand reputation, brand loyalty*, and *customer satisfaction* ratings can help assess the potential success of the investment. Additionally, reviewing *franchise agreements* and understanding the support and *marketing benefits* provided by the brand are important considerations.

Property condition assessment involves evaluating the physical condition of the hospitality building. This assessment includes *analyzing guest amenities*, such as room quality, public areas, and recreational facilities. Assessing the need for renovations or upgrades and estimating associated costs is crucial for budgeting and determining the potential return on investment.

Market analysis involves understanding the broader hospitality market trends and dynamics. This includes analyzing factors such as *local supply and demand, RevPAR trends*, and *market competition*. Conducting a competitor analysis helps identify the property's unique selling points and differentiators in the market.

By thoroughly evaluating these factors, investors can make informed decisions about hospitality building investments. A holistic analysis of location, financials, brand, property condition, and market trends helps mitigate risks and identify opportunities for maximizing returns. The ultimate goal is to select properties with strong market potential, revenue generation capabilities, and the potential for long-term growth and success in the hospitality industry.

12.4 Property Management and Guest Experience

Effective property management and delivering a positive guest experience are crucial for the success of hospitality properties. Key considerations in property management include operations and staffing, revenue management, guest satisfaction, marketing and promotions, as well as regulatory compliance and safety measures.

Operations and staffing considerations involve ensuring the smooth day-to-day operation of the property. This includes *staffing the property* with well-trained and competent personnel, such as front desk staff, housekeeping, maintenance, and food and beverage teams. *Efficient management of operations*, including check-in/check-out processes, housekeeping schedules, and maintenance procedures, is essential to provide a seamless experience for guests.

Revenue management and pricing strategies are important to maximize the property's revenue potential. This involves analyzing *market trends*, *demand patterns*, and *competitor pricing* to determine optimal room rates and pricing strategies. Employing revenue management techniques, such as *dynamic pricing*, promotional offers, and package deals, can help optimize occupancy rates and revenue generation.

Guest satisfaction and reviews management are critical for building a positive reputation and attracting repeat guests. Providing *exceptional* *customer service*, addressing guest concerns promptly, and ensuring a comfortable and enjoyable stay are key aspects of guest satisfaction. *Monitoring guest reviews* and feedback on online platforms and addressing them proactively can help maintain a positive image and address any areas for improvement.

Marketing and promotions play a vital role in attracting guests and increasing bookings. Effective marketing strategies may include *online and offline advertising, social media campaigns, partnerships with travel agents* or *online travel agencies*, and *loyalty programs*. A well-designed website with clear information and an easy booking process is also essential for driving direct bookings.

Regulatory compliance and safety measures are essential to ensure guest safety and meet legal requirements. This includes adhering to *local regulations* related to fire safety, food handling, health and hygiene, and accessibility. Implementing *security measures*, such as surveillance systems and staff training, is also important to provide a safe environment for guests.

Overall, effective property management and a positive guest experience are integral to the success of hospitality properties. By focusing on efficient operations, revenue management, guest satisfaction, marketing efforts, and compliance with regulations, investors can enhance the property's reputation, attract more guests, and generate higher revenues. Continuous monitoring and improvement in these areas are key to maintaining a competitive edge in the hospitality industry.

12.5 Risks and Rewards of Investing in Hospitality Buildings

Investing in hospitality buildings presents potential rewards, risks and challenges, risk mitigate and market factors. Case studies provide valuable insights into both successful and challenging investments in the hospitality sector. By understanding these dynamics and learning from case studies, investors can make informed decisions and navigate the risks and rewards associated with investing in hospitality buildings.

Potential rewards of investing in hospitality buildings include *revenue generation, capital appreciation,* and *brand value.* Well-managed properties with high occupancy rates and *strong average daily rates (ADR)* can generate significant income. Additionally, hospitality properties in desirable locations or those experiencing growth can *appreciate in value* over time. Investing in established brands or successfully building a reputable brand can enhance the property's value and market appeal.

Risks and challenges in the hospitality sector include *seasonality, economic factors,* and a *competitive landscape.*

1. *Seasonality* can lead to fluctuations in demand and revenue, particularly in tourist destinations or during off-peak travel periods.
2. *Economic factors* such as recessions or economic downturns can impact travel and leisure spending, affecting the performance of hospitality properties.
3. The *competitive landscape* is also a challenge, with numerous properties vying for guests and market share.

Mitigating risks in hospitality building investments involves *conducting thorough market research* to identify demand drivers and potential challenges. *Selecting a reputable and well-positioned brand* can provide support in marketing and guest acquisition. Effective *property management,* including revenue management strategies, guest satisfaction initiatives, and operational efficiency, is crucial for maximizing returns and minimizing risks.

Market factors that impact hospitality building investments include *travel trends* and *market competition.*

1. *Changes in travel patterns,* such as shifts towards experiential travel or increased demand for sustainable accommodations, can affect the desirability and profitability of hospitality properties.
2. Additionally, *market competition,* including the emergence of alternative accommodations like vacation rentals or home-sharing platforms, can impact occupancy rates and pricing dynamics.

Case studies of successful and challenging hospitality building investments provide valuable insights and lessons learned. These examples showcase strategies that have led to success, such as *repositioning underperforming properties,* implementing effective *marketing and branding initiatives,* or capitalizing on unique market niches. They also highlight challenges faced by investors, such as overcoming financial hurdles, managing property renovations, or adapting to changing market dynamics.

In conclusion, investing in hospitality buildings offers potential rewards in terms of revenue generation, capital appreciation, and brand value. However, risks related to seasonality, economic factors, and market competition must be carefully managed. Conducting market research, selecting the right brand, and implementing effective property management strategies are key to mitigating risks and maximizing returns. Staying informed about market factors and learning from case studies can further inform investment decisions in the hospitality sector.

Conclusion

Investing in private equity real estate hospitality buildings requires a comprehensive understanding of key concepts and terminologies. By recapitulating these concepts and emphasizing the importance of analysis and guest experience management, investors can make informed decisions and maximize the potential of their investments. Thorough analysis of location, financials, brand, property condition, and market trends provides valuable insights for making informed decisions. Attention to guest experience management enhances the property's reputation, guest satisfaction, and revenue generation potential. Ultimately, successful investments in private equity real estate hospitality buildings depend on a thorough understanding of the industry, meticulous analysis, and a commitment to delivering exceptional guest experiences.

Chapter 13: Investing in Private Equity Real Estate Funds

Instead of creating your own Private Equity Firm, you could invest in a variety of other people's real estate funds.

Real Estate Fund - Photo by Joshua Mayo

13.1 What are Real Estate Funds?

Real estate funds are investment vehicles that **pool capital from multiple investors** to invest in real estate assets. This section provides an overview of real estate funds, including their definition, structure, and characteristics. Real estate funds serve the purpose of facilitating private equity investments in the real estate sector, offering opportunities for diversification and potential returns. Real estate funds are essential components of diversified investment portfolios, providing exposure to the real estate market and potential long-term growth.

Real estate funds are investment vehicles that pool together capital from multiple investors to invest in a portfolio of real estate assets. These funds provide individuals and institutional investors with the opportunity to access the real estate market without directly owning properties. Real estate funds can take various forms, including *private equity real estate funds, real estate investment trusts (REITs)*, and *real estate mutual funds*.

Real estate funds typically have a specific investment strategy and focus, such as *residential properties, commercial buildings*, or *specific geographic regions*. They are managed by **professional fund managers** who make investment decisions on behalf of the fund and oversee the fund's operations.

The structure and characteristics of real estate funds vary depending on the type of fund. Private equity real estate funds are typically **closed-end funds**, meaning they have a fixed lifespan and a limited number of investors. These funds raise capital through *private placements* and have a specific investment strategy and targeted return goals.

Real estate investment trusts (REITs), on the other hand, are publicly traded companies that own and operate income-generating properties. They are required to *distribute a significant portion* of their taxable income to shareholders in the form of *dividends*.

Real estate mutual funds are open-end funds that allow investors to *buy and sell shares* at the net asset value (NAV) of the fund. These funds invest in a diversified portfolio of real estate securities, such as *REITs, real estate stocks*, and *mortgage-backed securities*.

The purpose of real estate funds in private equity investing is to provide investors with **exposure to the real estate market** and the potential for income generation and capital appreciation. These funds allow investors to diversify their portfolios, as real estate investments often have different risk and return characteristics compared to traditional asset classes such as stocks and bonds.

Fund managers play a crucial role in the operations of real estate funds. They are responsible for sourcing and evaluating investment opportunities, executing transactions, managing the fund's portfolio, and providing regular reporting to investors. Fund managers leverage their expertise and market knowledge to make informed investment decisions and optimize the performance of the fund.

In summary, real estate funds are investment vehicles that allow investors to gain exposure to the real estate market. These funds are structured differently depending on the type, and they serve the purpose of diversifying investment portfolios and providing potential income and capital appreciation. Fund managers play a critical role in managing the operations and performance of the fund. Including real estate funds in an investment portfolio can contribute to long-term wealth accumulation and risk management.

13.2 Types of Real Estate Funds

Real estate funds come in various types, each with its own investment strategy and focus. Here are some common types of real estate funds:

1. **Core Funds:** These funds invest in *stable, income-generating properties* with a focus on preserving capital and generating consistent cash flows. Core funds typically target *well-established properties* in prime locations with high occupancy rates and long-term leases. The primary objective of core funds is to provide steady income and moderate capital appreciation.
2. **Value-Added Funds:** Value-added funds seek properties that have the potential for *value enhancement* through

renovations, repositioning, or operational improvements. These funds aim to *increase property value* and cash flows by actively managing and improving the assets. Value-added funds may target properties with occupancy or management issues, with the goal of increasing rents, attracting higher-quality tenants, or improving operational efficiencies.

3. **Opportunistic Funds:** Opportunistic funds pursue high-risk, *high-reward* investments in undervalued or distressed properties. These funds take advantage of market inefficiencies, economic downturns, or property-specific challenges to *acquire assets at discounted prices.* The investment strategy of opportunistic funds often involves significant repositioning, redevelopment, or restructuring of properties to generate substantial returns.

4. **Sector-Specific Funds:** Sector-specific funds focus on specific segments of the real estate market, such as *residential, commercial, industrial,* or *hospitality* properties. These funds specialize in a particular property type and leverage their expertise and market knowledge to identify and invest in opportunities within their chosen sector. Sector-specific funds allow investors to target their investments in areas they believe have the most potential for growth and profitability.

5. **Geographically Focused Funds:** Geographically focused funds concentrate their investments in *specific regions,* countries, or even international markets. These funds capitalize on *localized market trends, economic conditions,* and growth potential in specific geographic areas. Geographically focused funds allow investors to diversify their real estate portfolios across different regions or focus on markets they believe offer the best opportunities.

Each type of real estate fund has its own risk and return profile, investment horizon, and targeted investor base. It's important for investors to understand the characteristics and objectives of each fund type before making investment decisions. Diversifying across different types of real estate funds can provide a well-rounded exposure to the real estate market and help manage risk within a portfolio.

13.3 Advantages and Disadvantages of Investing in Real Estate Funds

Investing in real estate funds offers several advantages, but there are also some disadvantages that investors should consider. Here are the key advantages and disadvantages of investing in real estate funds:

Advantages

1. *Professional Management:* Real estate funds are managed by experienced professionals who have expertise in *property selection*, *acquisition*, and *asset management*. Investors can benefit from the knowledge and skills of the fund managers, who make informed investment decisions on behalf of the fund.

2. *Diversification:* Real estate funds provide access to a diversified portfolio of properties across different types, sectors, and geographies. This diversification helps reduce risk by *spreading investments across multiple assets*, thereby potentially reducing the impact of a single property's performance on the overall investment.

3. *Access to Institutional-Grade Properties:* Real estate funds often invest in *high-quality, institutional-grade properties* that may be difficult for individual investors to access directly. By investing in a fund, individual investors gain exposure to these properties and benefit from the potential income

generation and capital appreciation they offer.

Disadvantages

1. *Limited Control:* Investing in a real estate fund means giving up direct control over investment decisions. *Fund managers make all the investment choices*, and investors have little say in the specific properties or projects selected. This lack of control can be a disadvantage for investors who prefer to have direct involvement in their investment decisions.

2. *Lock-Up Periods:* Real estate funds typically have lock-up periods, during which investors are *unable to withdraw their capital.* These lock-up periods can range from several years to a decade or more, depending on the fund's structure and strategy. Investors need to consider their liquidity needs and the potential impact of lock-up periods on their investment strategy.

3. *Fees and Expenses:* Real estate funds charge fees and expenses, including *management fees, performance fees,* and *operational expenses.* These fees can eat into the overall investment returns and should be carefully considered by investors. It's important to understand the fee structure and assess the potential impact on the investment's profitability.

Other Considerations

1. *Potential for Regular Income Distribution and Capital Appreciation:* Real estate funds often distribute *regular income* to investors in the form of *dividends* or distributions from rental income. Additionally, investors may benefit from capital appreciation as property values increase over time. These potential income streams make real estate funds attractive to investors seeking regular cash flow.

2. *Fund Performance and Track Record:* Evaluating the *historical performance* and *track record* of a real estate fund is essential. Investors should assess factors such as *past returns, consistency of performance,* and the fund's ability to achieve its *stated objectives.* A strong track record and positive performance can provide confidence in the fund's investment strategy and management capabilities.

3. *Alignment of Interests:* It's important to consider the alignment of interests between fund managers and investors. Look for funds where the managers have a significant personal investment in the fund, as this aligns their interests with those of the investors. This alignment ensures that the fund managers are motivated to generate positive returns and act in the best interests of the investors.

In summary, investing in real estate funds offers advantages such as professional management, diversification, and access to institutional-grade properties. However, there are disadvantages such as limited control, lock-up periods, and fees. Considerations of regular income distribution, fund performance, and alignment of interests are important factors for investors to evaluate before investing in real estate funds.

13.4 How to Evaluate Real Estate Funds

When evaluating real estate funds, there are several key factors to consider. Here are the important aspects to assess:

1. **Fund Strategy and Investment Objectives:** Understand the fund's investment strategy, target market, and property types. Evaluate if the fund's objectives align with your investment goals and risk tolerance. Consider factors such as the fund's focus on *income generation, capital appreciation,* or *value-add*

opportunities.

2. **Fund Performance Metrics:** Examine key performance metrics such as the *net asset value (NAV)* and *internal rate of return (IRR)* of the fund. Assess how the fund has performed in comparison to its stated objectives and benchmarks. Analyze the historical performance over different market cycles to evaluate consistency and resilience.

3. **Track Record and Experience of Fund Managers:** Evaluate the track record and *experience of the fund managers*. Assess their expertise in real estate investing, including their success in managing similar funds or investments. Look for managers with a *proven ability to generate attractive risk-adjusted returns* and a history of successful exits.

4. **Fund Portfolio Analysis:** Analyze the fund's portfolio composition, including *property types*, *geographic distribution*, and *tenant mix*. Assess if the portfolio aligns with the fund's strategy and objectives. Consider factors such as property quality, occupancy rates, lease terms, and tenant diversification. A well-diversified portfolio across property types and locations can help mitigate risk.

5. **Due Diligence on Fund Financials, Valuations, and Legal Documentation:** Conduct thorough due diligence on the fund's financials, valuations, and legal documentation. Review *audited financial statements*, *valuation reports*, and *investor communications*. Assess the fund's fee structure, expenses, and any potential conflicts of interest. Review legal documents, such as the offering memorandum or prospectus, to understand the fund's terms and conditions.

Additionally, it is recommended to **seek advice from professional advisors,** such as financial consultants or legal experts, who specialize in real estate fund investments. They can help analyze the fund's *structure*, *performance*, and *documentation*, and provide insights to support your decision-making process.

By evaluating these factors, investors can make informed decisions when selecting real estate funds. It's important to conduct thorough due diligence and assess the fund's strategy, performance, management team, portfolio, and financials to ensure alignment with your investment objectives and risk tolerance.

13.5 Risks Associated with Investing in Real Estate Funds

Investing in real estate funds involves various risks that investors should be aware of. Here are the key risks associated with investing in real estate funds:

1. **Market and Economic Risks Impacting Fund Performance:** Real estate funds are influenced by market and economic conditions. Factors such as changes in *interest rates*, *GDP growth*, and *consumer confidence* can affect property valuations, occupancy rates, and rental income. Economic downturns or recessions can lead to decreased property demand and rental income, impacting the fund's performance.

2. **Property Market Cycles and Market Timing Risks**: Real estate markets go through cycles of *expansion*, *peak*, *contraction*, and *recovery*. *Timing the market* correctly can be challenging, and investing during the wrong phase of the cycle may lead to suboptimal returns. Property values can fluctuate, and investing at the peak of a cycle may result in overpaying for assets.

3. **Liquidity Risks and Limited Exit Options:** Real estate investments typically have *longer investment horizons* and *limited liquidity* compared to other asset classes. Real estate

funds often have lock-up periods, restricting investors' ability to exit their investments during specific time frames. In addition, the real estate market may experience *periods of illiquidity*, making it challenging to sell properties or redeem investments when desired.

4. **Regulatory and Compliance Risks:** Real estate investments are subject to regulatory requirements and compliance obligations. Changes in *regulations, zoning laws, tax policies*, or *environmental regulations* can impact property values and operating costs. Non-compliance with regulations can result in *financial penalties* or restrictions on property use. Investors should consider the regulatory and compliance risks associated with real estate investments.

5. **Mitigating Risks:**

    1. *Portfolio Diversification:* Diversifying across different *property types, sectors*, and *geographic locations* can help reduce the impact of individual property or market-specific risks. A well-diversified real estate portfolio can help mitigate the effects of localized market downturns and enhance overall risk-adjusted returns.

    2. *Active Management:* Engaging skilled and experienced fund managers who actively manage the properties within the fund can help mitigate risks. Active management involves monitoring market conditions, implementing effective property management strategies, and making timely decisions to optimize performance. Proactive measures can help address potential risks and enhance returns.

It's important for investors to thoroughly assess the risks associated with real estate funds and consider their risk tolerance and investment objectives before making investment decisions. Conducting proper due diligence, staying informed about market conditions, and diversifying investments can help mitigate risks and enhance the likelihood of achieving investment goals.

Conclusion

In conclusion, investing in private equity real estate funds offers the potential benefits of professional management, diversification, and access to attractive real estate investments. It is crucial for investors to conduct thorough due diligence, assess the fund's strategy, performance, and portfolio, and ensure alignment with their investment objectives. By doing so, investors can make informed decisions and enhance the likelihood of achieving their investment goals in the real estate sector.

Chapter 14: Private Equity Crowdfunding

Instead of creating your own Private Equity Firm, you could invest in a variety of other people's projects through crowdfunding platforms.

14.1 What is Private Equity Crowdfunding?

Private equity crowdfunding refers to the practice of raising capital from a large number of individuals, typically through an **online platform**, to invest in private equity projects, including real estate. Here is an overview of private equity crowdfunding and its role in real estate investing:

1. **Definition and Overview:** Private equity crowdfunding involves pooling funds from multiple investors, often through an *online platform*, to invest in private equity opportunities, such as *real estate projects*. It provides individuals with access to investment opportunities that were traditionally available

only to institutional investors or high-net-worth individuals.

2. **Role in Real Estate Investing:** Private equity crowdfunding has gained popularity in the real estate sector as it enables investors to participate in real estate projects with *lower minimum investment requirements*. It allows individuals to diversify their investment portfolios by accessing a *range of real estate opportunities*, including residential, commercial, and hospitality properties.

3. **Key Features and Mechanics:** Private equity crowdfunding platforms provide a *marketplace* where investors can browse and *select investment opportunities*. Investors can review project details, including property information, financial projections, and expected returns. They can then invest a specified amount in the project, typically in exchange for equity or debt instruments. Investors may receive regular updates on the project's progress and potential distributions.

4. **Regulatory Considerations and Legal Framework:** Private equity crowdfunding is subject to regulatory considerations and legal frameworks that vary by jurisdiction. The same securities laws and regulations previously mentioned govern the offering and sale of securities through crowdfunding platforms. Platforms must comply with investor protection measures and adhere to rules regarding fundraising, disclosure, and reporting. Regulations such as the JOBS Act in the United States have facilitated the growth of private equity crowdfunding by creating exemptions and streamlining the process for certain offerings.

5. **Evolution and Growth:** The private equity crowdfunding industry has experienced significant growth in recent years, driven by advancements in technology, regulatory changes, and increasing investor interest. Crowdfunding platforms have expanded globally, offering investors a wide range of real

estate investment opportunities. The industry continues to evolve, with platforms adopting innovative structures, introducing secondary markets, and enhancing investor protections.

Private equity crowdfunding has democratized access to private equity investments, allowing a broader range of investors to participate in real estate projects. However, it's important for investors to conduct thorough due diligence on crowdfunding platforms, evaluate investment opportunities, and understand the associated risks before making investment decisions. Regulatory compliance and investor protections are essential considerations for both platforms and investors participating in private equity crowdfunding.

14.2 Types of Private Equity Crowdfunding

Private equity crowdfunding encompasses various models and structures that cater to different investor preferences and project needs. Here are the main types of private equity crowdfunding:

1. **Equity-Based Crowdfunding:** In this model, investors provide capital in exchange for equity ownership in the project or company. *Investors become shareholders* and may benefit from potential *capital appreciation* and *dividends*. Equity-based crowdfunding is commonly used in real estate, allowing investors to participate in the ownership and potential profits of real estate projects.

2. **Debt-Based Crowdfunding:** This model involves *investors providing loans* or debt instruments to the project or company. Investors earn interest on their investment and receive regular repayments over a specified period. Debt-based crowdfunding is often utilized for real estate projects where investors act as lenders, providing financing to

developers or property owners.

3. **Reward-Based Crowdfunding:** In reward-based crowdfunding, investors contribute funds to a project and receive *non-equity rewards or perks* in return. These rewards can vary depending on the project and may include early access to products, exclusive experiences, or other tangible benefits. While reward-based crowdfunding is more common in creative projects or startups, it can also be used in real estate for unique offerings, such as vacation rentals or hospitality experiences.

4. **Hybrid Models and Alternative Structures:** Private equity crowdfunding can also involve hybrid models or alternative structures that *combine elements of equity, debt, and rewards.* For example, revenue-sharing models provide investors with a share of the project's revenue or profits. Other structures may include profit-sharing arrangements or preferred equity, which offer investors specific rights and priority in distributions.

5. **Specialized Crowdfunding Platforms for Real Estate:** Given the popularity of real estate crowdfunding, specialized platforms have emerged that focus exclusively on real estate projects. These platforms provide a *marketplace for investors* to discover and invest in a range of real estate opportunities. They often offer features such as due diligence reports, project information, and investor dashboards to facilitate investment decision-making.

It's important for investors to understand the specific terms, risks, and potential returns associated with each crowdfunding model before making investment decisions. *Due diligence*, including evaluating the project, its sponsors, and the crowdfunding platform, is essential to assess the viability and credibility of the investment opportunity.

Investors should also consider their risk tolerance, investment objectives, and the potential liquidity of their investments in private equity crowdfunding.

14.3 Advantages and Disadvantages of Private Equity Crowdfunding

Private equity crowdfunding offers several **advantages and benefits** for investors, but it also comes with certain disadvantages and risks. Here is an overview of the advantages and disadvantages of private equity crowdfunding:

Advantages

1. **Access to Investment Opportunities:** Private equity crowdfunding provides individual investors with *access to a wide range of investment opportunities* that were traditionally available only to institutional investors or high-net-worth individuals. Investors can choose from various projects and industries, including real estate, and diversify their portfolios.

2. **Diversification:** Private equity crowdfunding allows investors to diversify their investment portfolios by *spreading their capital across multiple projects* or companies. This diversification helps mitigate risks associated with individual investments and industries, potentially enhancing overall portfolio performance.

3. **Lower Investment Minimums:** Crowdfunding platforms often have lower investment minimums compared to traditional private equity investments. This enables investors with smaller capital to *participate in projects* they find attractive, including real estate developments, without the need for substantial upfront investments.

4. **Democratization of Investing:** Private equity crowdfunding

democratizes the investment landscape by providing opportunities for a *broader range of investors* to participate in private equity investments. It promotes inclusivity and allows individuals to invest in projects aligned with their interests and goals.

5. **Potential for Higher Returns and Passive Income Generation**: Private equity investments, including real estate projects, have the potential to generate higher returns compared to traditional asset classes. Investors can benefit from capital appreciation, dividends, rental income, or profit-sharing arrangements, which can contribute to passive income generation.

Disadvantages

1. **Limited Control:** Investors in private equity crowdfunding typically have limited control and influence over the management and decision-making of the invested project or company. Major *decisions are typically made by the project sponsor* or management team, and investors may have little say in the day-to-day operations.
2. **Liquidity Constraints:** Private equity crowdfunding investments are often illiquid, meaning that investors may have *limited opportunities to sell* their shares or exit their investments before the project's completion or maturity. This lack of liquidity can tie up capital for an extended period, limiting investors' access to their funds.
3. **Regulatory Risks:** Crowdfunding activities are subject to regulatory frameworks and compliance requirements that vary by jurisdiction. Changes in regulations or legal restrictions can impact the crowdfunding landscape, potentially affecting investor rights, platform operations, and the overall crowdfunding environment.

Risk Factors and Due Diligence Considerations

Investing in private equity crowdfunding involves certain risk factors and requires careful due diligence. Investors should consider factors such as:

- **Project or Company Risk:** Assessing the *project's or company's viability, financial projections, market potential,* and *competitive landscape* is crucial to evaluate the investment's risk and potential returns.
- **Platform Due Diligence:** Evaluating the credibility and reputation of the crowdfunding platform is essential. Investors should *review the platform's track record, security measures, investor protections*, and *compliance* with regulations.
- **Risk Mitigation:** Diversification across multiple investments, conducting thorough due diligence, and understanding the associated risks are key to mitigating potential risks in private equity crowdfunding.

Overall, private equity crowdfunding can provide investors with access to investment opportunities, diversification, and potential returns. However, it is important for investors to carefully assess the risks, perform due diligence, and consider their investment objectives and risk tolerance before participating in private equity crowdfunding.

14.4 How to Evaluate Private Equity Crowdfunding

Private equity crowdfunding has gained significant popularity as a means for entrepreneurs and small businesses to raise capital. However, evaluating such investments requires a thorough analysis of various factors.

1. One crucial aspect is the **assessment of the project or company** seeking funding. This evaluation typically involves scrutinizing the business plan, financial projections, and management team. By carefully examining these elements, potential investors can gain insights into the viability and potential profitability of the venture.
   1. The *business plan* provides a comprehensive overview of the company's goals, strategies, and market positioning.
   2. *Financial projections* allow investors to assess the projected revenues, expenses, and potential returns on investment.
   3. *Evaluating the management team's* qualifications, experience, and track record helps gauge their ability to execute the business plan effectively.
2. Another essential aspect of evaluating private equity crowdfunding is conducting a **risk assessment** and **identifying mitigation strategies**. Risks can include *market volatility, industry-specific challenges, competition, regulatory changes*, and *operational* risks. It is essential to assess the likelihood and potential impact of these risks. Mitigation strategies, such as diversification, contingency planning, and risk management techniques, can help investors navigate potential challenges and minimize the negative impact of risks.
3. When considering private equity crowdfunding opportunities, platform **due diligence** is crucial. Investors should evaluate the *reputation and track record of the crowdfunding platform itself*. This involves assessing the platform's history, success rate in funding projects, and its ability to attract reputable and high-quality ventures. Additionally, investor protections provided by the platform,

such as clear terms and conditions, dispute resolution mechanisms, and transparency in investment processes, are crucial considerations.

4. **Legal and regulatory compliance** review is another vital aspect of evaluating private equity crowdfunding opportunities. Investors must ensure that the project or company seeking funding *complies with applicable laws and regulations*. This review includes assessing the project's legal structure, licensing requirements, compliance with securities regulations, and adherence to investor protection laws. Engaging legal professionals with expertise in crowdfunding and securities regulations can be beneficial in conducting a thorough compliance review.

5. Lastly, investors should consider **investor rights, reporting mechanisms, and exit strategies** when evaluating private equity crowdfunding opportunities. This includes assessing the *terms of the investment* agreement, the level of transparency in reporting financial and operational performance, and the mechanisms in place for investor communication and engagement. Additionally, evaluating the potential exit strategies is crucial for determining the liquidity and potential returns on investment. Common exit strategies include *initial public offerings (IPOs)*, *acquisitions*, or *buybacks*.

In conclusion, thorough evaluation of private equity crowdfunding opportunities entails analyzing business plans, financial projections, and management teams. Mitigating risks and assessing the reputation of crowdfunding platforms are essential. Legal compliance, investor rights, reporting mechanisms, and exit strategies must be considered for a comprehensive understanding. By taking these factors into account, investors can make informed decisions and enhance their chances of success in private equity crowdfunding.

14.5 Popular Private Equity Crowdfunding Platforms

While there are numerous crowdfunding platforms in the private equity space, here is an overview of some leading platforms specifically focused on real estate:

1. **RealtyShares:** RealtyShares offers a wide range of real estate investment opportunities, including residential, commercial, and industrial properties. Investors can browse projects, review financials and projections, and invest in properties with varying investment minimums.

2. **Fundrise:** Fundrise provides access to a diversified portfolio of real estate assets, including residential, commercial, and mixed-use properties. Investors can choose from different investment plans based on their risk tolerance and investment goals. Fundrise also offers eREITs, which are electronically traded real estate investment trusts.

3. **PeerStreet:** PeerStreet specializes in debt-based real estate crowdfunding, focusing on short-term, high-yield loans secured by real estate. Investors can participate in fractional investments in real estate-backed loans, with the platform conducting thorough due diligence on each loan opportunity.

4. **RealtyMogul:** RealtyMogul offers a range of real estate investment opportunities, including equity and debt investments. Investors can select from various property types, such as multifamily, office, retail, and hospitality. The platform provides detailed property information, financial projections, and historical performance data to assist investors in their decision-making process.

5. **Crowdstreet:** The platform offers a range of investment options, including equity investments, preferred equity, and debt investments. The platform allows investors to browse and review a variety of real estate deals across different asset classes, such as multifamily properties, office buildings, retail spaces, and industrial properties.

Choosing the right crowdfunding platform depends on several factors, including investment preferences, risk tolerance, and desired level of involvement. Considerations for selecting a platform include:

1. **Investment Offerings:** Evaluate the types of investment opportunities offered by the platform, such as equity or debt investments, specific property types, and geographic locations. Ensure that the platform aligns with your investment goals and preferences.
2. **Platform Features and Transparency:** Look for platforms that provide comprehensive project details, financial projections, due diligence reports, and investor dashboards. Transparency in communication, regular updates, and access to project information are important factors to consider.
3. **Investor Requirements:** Review the minimum investment amounts, eligibility criteria, and accreditation requirements of the platform. Some platforms may require investors to meet specific income or net worth thresholds to participate.

Case studies of successful projects or companies funded through crowdfunding can provide insights into the platform's track record and potential returns. Analyzing the performance of past projects, the level of investor satisfaction, and the platform's ability to deliver on its promises is essential.

The future outlook of private equity crowdfunding is positive, with continued growth expected. Technology advancements, regulatory changes, and increasing investor interest in alternative investments are likely to contribute to the expansion of the crowdfunding industry. However, regulatory developments and evolving market conditions will influence the dynamics of the crowdfunding space. It is important for investors to stay informed about trends, platform performance, and regulatory updates to make informed investment decisions in the evolving landscape of private equity crowdfunding.

Conclusion

In conclusion, this chapter explored private equity crowdfunding in real estate investing, highlighting its democratizing effect by providing access to investment opportunities previously reserved for institutional investors. It covered the mechanics of crowdfunding platforms, regulatory considerations, and different crowdfunding models. The chapter outlines the advantages of private equity crowdfunding, such as increased access and diversification, while acknowledging the disadvantages, such as limited control and regulatory risks. It provides guidelines for evaluating crowdfunding opportunities, including due diligence and compliance assessment. The chapter concludes with popular platforms and mentions the future growth potential of private equity crowdfunding driven by technology, regulations, and investor interest. Overall, it offers a comprehensive understanding of private equity crowdfunding in real estate and serves as a guide for evaluating opportunities in this alternative investment method.

Chapter 15: Understanding Real Estate Investment Trusts (REITs)

Instead of creating your own Private Equity Firm, another way you could invest in a variety of REITs.

15.1 What are REITs?

In this section, we delve into the world of Real Estate Investment Trusts (REITs) and explore their fundamental aspects and significance in private equity real estate investments. We beging by providing a comprehensive definition and overview of REITs, shedding light on their unique characteristics and structure and then delve into the legal requirements and tax treatment associated with REITs. Next, we examine the purpose and objectives of REITs in the real estate market, and finally, we emphasize the importance of REITs in private equity real estate investments.

A **Real Estate Investment Trust (REIT)** is a type of company that owns, operates, or finances income-generating real estate properties. REITs allow individual investors to invest in real estate *without directly owning or managing the properties*. Here is an overview of REITs:

Definition and Overview: REITs are publicly traded companies that pool investors' capital to invest in a diversified portfolio of real estate assets. These assets can include *commercial properties* (office buildings, shopping malls, hotels), *residential properties* (apartment complexes), *industrial properties* (warehouses, distribution centers), and other types of income-producing real estate.

Structure and Characteristics: REITs are structured as corporations, trusts, or associations and are managed by a *board of directors or trustees*. They issue shares to investors, who become *shareholders* of the REIT. REITs are required by law to *distribute a significant portion of their taxable income* (usually at least 90%) to shareholders in the form of dividends.

Legal Requirements and Tax Treatment: To qualify as a REIT, a company must meet certain legal requirements. For example, in the United States, REITs must have

1. at least 75% of their assets invested in real estate,
2. derive at least 75% of their income from real estate activities, and
3. distribute at least 90% of their taxable income to shareholders.

In return, REITs enjoy *favorable tax treatment*, such as exemption from corporate income tax, provided they meet the specified criteria.

Purpose and Objectives: The primary purpose of REITs is to generate income and provide a means for investors to *participate in the real* *estate market.* REITs allow individual investors to access real estate investments that would otherwise require significant capital and expertise. They offer a way to invest in a *diversified portfolio* of real estate assets and benefit from potential income and capital appreciation.

Importance in Private Equity Real Estate Investments: REITs play a significant role in private equity real estate investments by *providing liquidity and diversification* opportunities. They allow investors to allocate capital to real estate as an asset class while enjoying the benefits of professional management and the ability to easily buy and sell shares on public exchanges. REITs also provide access to a *broader range of properties and markets*, including sectors that may be challenging for individual investors to enter.

REITs have become a popular investment vehicle, attracting a wide range of investors, including individuals, institutional investors, and pension funds. They offer the potential for regular income, portfolio diversification, and exposure to the real estate market. However, investors should carefully evaluate the specific REIT's strategy, management team, and financial performance before making investment decisions.

15.2 Types of REITs

By understanding the nuances of each type, investors can navigate the REIT landscape effectively and tailor their investment strategies to align with their financial objectives and preferences. In this section, we delve into the world of Real Estate Investment Trusts (REITs) and their **diverse types.** REITs offer investors unique opportunities in the real estate market, with a focus on income-generating properties, mortgage financing, or a combination of both. We explore *Equity REITs*, which involve ownership and operation of income-generating properties, *Mortgage REITs* specializing in mortgage financing, and *Hybrid REITs* that combine characteristics of both. We also compare Publicly Traded

REITs and Non-Traded REITs, and highlight the significance of *Specialized REITs* targeting specific sectors like healthcare, retail, industrial, and residential.

There are several types of REITs that cater to different aspects of the real estate market. Here are the main categories:

1. **Equity REITs:** Equity REITs are the most common type of REITs. They own and operate *income-generating properties*, such as *office buildings, shopping malls, apartment complexes,* and *industrial facilities.* These REITs generate *rental income from leasing* out the properties to tenants. Investors in equity REITs earn returns through *dividends* from the rental income and potential capital appreciation of the underlying properties.

2. **Mortgage REITs:** Mortgage REITs focus on financing real estate by investing in *mortgages and mortgage-backed securities.* Rather than owning physical properties, they *provide loans to real estate owners* or *invest in mortgage securities.* Mortgage REITs generate income from *interest payments* on the mortgages they hold. These REITs may be exposed to interest rate risks and credit risks associated with the mortgages in their portfolios.

3. **Hybrid REITs:** Hybrid REITs combine characteristics of both equity and mortgage REITs. They *own and operate properties,* as well as *invest in mortgages* and mortgage-backed securities. This combination *allows them to diversify* their revenue streams and potentially mitigate certain risks associated with either type of investment. Hybrid REITs offer a *balanced approach* to real estate investing by including both equity ownership and mortgage financing in their portfolios.

4. **Publicly Traded REITs vs. Non-Traded REITs:**
   1. *Publicly traded REITs* are *listed on stock exchanges*

      and can be bought and sold like regular stocks. They provide investors with *liquidity and daily price transparency*.

2. *Non-traded REITs*, on the other hand, are not publicly traded and do not have a readily available market for their shares. Non-traded REITs typically have a fixed period during which investors can redeem their shares, but *liquidity is generally limited*. Non-traded REITs may offer *higher dividend yields* but involve *longer holding periods* and less price transparency.

5. **Specialized REITs:** Specialized REITs focus on specific sectors or property types within the real estate market. Examples include *healthcare REITs* that own and lease healthcare facilities, *retail REITs* that specialize in shopping centers and retail properties, *industrial REITs* that invest in warehouses and distribution centers, and *residential REITs* that focus on rental housing properties. Specialized REITs allow investors to target specific sectors based on their investment preferences and market outlook.

Investors should consider their investment goals, risk tolerance, and market conditions when choosing among the different types of REITs. Each type offers unique exposure to the real estate market and comes with its own benefits and considerations. It's important to conduct thorough research and due diligence on specific REITs, including their financial performance, property portfolio, management team, and investment strategy, before making investment decisions.

15.3 How REITs Differ from Other Real Estate Investments

In this section, we explore how Real Estate Investment Trusts (REITs) **differ from other forms of real estate investments**. We examine key factors that set REITs apart, including the liquidity and market accessibility of REIT investments, the advantages of professional management and diversification in REITs, the passive ownership structure of REITs, the income distribution and dividends that REITs provide to shareholders, and the reporting and regulatory requirements imposed on REITs helps investors assess the unique benefits and considerations of REIT investments compared to other real estate investment options.

REITs offer distinct advantages and characteristics that differentiate them from other types of real estate investments. Here are the key differences:

1. **Liquidity and Market Accessibility:** REITs are *publicly traded on stock exchanges*, providing investors with *liquidity* and the *ability to buy and sell shares* on a daily basis. This makes REITs more accessible compared to directly owning physical properties, which can be illiquid and require a longer time to sell. The public market for REIT shares provides *price transparency* and the opportunity for investors to adjust their positions easily.

2. **Professional Management and Diversification:** REITs are managed by professional teams with *expertise in real estate investment* and *property management*. These teams handle the day-to-day operations, tenant leasing, and property maintenance. By investing in a REIT, individuals benefit from the professional management of a diversified portfolio of properties across different locations and sectors. This

diversification helps *spread risk* and *reduces exposure* to the performance of a single property.

3. **Passive Ownership and Shareholder Benefits:** Investing in REITs allows individuals to participate as passive owners of real estate. They *do not have to deal with the responsibilities of property management*, tenant relations, or ongoing maintenance. Additionally, REIT shareholders may receive benefits such as *regular income distributions* in the form of *dividends*, which are generated from the rental income or other earnings of the REIT.

4. **Income Distribution and Dividends:** One of the key features of REITs is their requirement to *distribute a significant portion of their taxable income to shareholders in the form of dividends*. This makes REITs attractive to income-oriented investors who seek regular cash flows from their investments. Dividends from REITs can provide a *consistent income* stream and may offer favorable tax treatment for investors.

5. **Reporting and Regulatory Requirements:** REITs are subject to specific reporting and regulatory requirements. They must comply with rules and regulations *set by the securities regulators* in the countries where they are listed. This includes providing regular *financial reports, disclosures* about their property portfolio, and adherence to specific criteria to maintain their REIT status. These requirements provide transparency and accountability to investors.

While REITs offer advantages such as liquidity, professional management, and income distribution, they also come with their own considerations. Investors should carefully assess factors such as the performance and track record of the REIT, the quality of the underlying properties, the expertise of the management team, and the prevailing market conditions before investing in REITs.

15.4 Advantages and Disadvantages of Investing in REITs

Investing in REITs has its advantages and disadvantages. On the positive side, REITs offer portfolio diversification, access to commercial real estate, and professional management. However, there are also downsides, including market volatility, reliance on real estate market performance, and limited control over property decisions. It's important to consider dividend income and potential capital appreciation when investing in REITs. Additionally, there are risk factors to be aware of, such as interest rate risks, economic conditions, and property market risks. By weighing these factors, investors can make informed decisions about their REIT investments.

Investing in REITs offers several advantages, but it's important to consider the associated disadvantages and risk factors. Here are the key points:

Advantages of Investing in REITs:

1. *Portfolio Diversification:* REITs allow investors to diversify their portfolios by gaining exposure to a wide range of commercial real estate properties across different *sectors, locations,* and *property types.* This diversification can help *reduce risk* and potentially enhance overall portfolio performance.
2. *Access to Commercial Real Estate:* Investing in REITs provides individuals with access to the commercial real estate market, which may otherwise require significant capital and expertise to enter as a direct investor. REITs enable investors to participate in income-generating properties such as *office buildings, shopping centers, apartments,* and *hotels.*

3. *Professional Management:* REITs are managed by experienced real estate professionals who handle *property acquisition, leasing, maintenance,* and other operational aspects. Investors can benefit from the expertise and resources of these professionals, which may lead to better property selection, improved performance, and efficient management of the portfolio.

Disadvantages of Investing in REITs:

1. *Market Volatility:* REIT prices can be subject to market volatility, influenced by factors such as *changes in interest rates, economic conditions,* and *investor sentiment.* This volatility may result in *fluctuations in the value of the investment* and potential capital losses.
2. *Dependency on Real Estate Market Performance:* REITs are directly affected by the performance of the underlying real estate market. Economic downturns, *changes in property demand,* and other market factors can impact the *rental income, occupancy rates,* and *property values* of the REIT's portfolio. Consequently, the performance of a REIT is closely tied to the overall health of the real estate market.
3. *Limited Control over Property Decisions:* As a REIT investor, you have limited control over property-specific decisions such as tenant selection, property improvements, and property management strategies. The *decision-making authority lies with the REIT's management team.* This lack of control may not suit investors who prefer a more hands-on approach to property investment.

Considerations in REIT Investments:

1. *Dividend Income and Potential Capital Appreciation:* REITs

typically distribute a significant portion of their taxable income to shareholders in the form of *dividends*. This regular income can be attractive to income-oriented investors. Additionally, REIT investments offer the potential for *capital appreciation* if the underlying properties increase in value over time.

2. *Risk Factors in REIT Investments:* Investors should be aware of the various risks associated with investing in REITs. *Interest rate risks*, *economic conditions*, and *property market risks* can impact the performance of REITs.

    1. *Rising interest rates* may increase borrowing costs for REITs, affecting their profitability.
    2. *Economic downturns* can reduce property demand and occupancy rates.
    3. *Property market risks* include changes in property values, supply and demand dynamics, and changes in rental rates.

It's essential for investors to carefully evaluate the specific REIT, its investment strategy, the quality of its property portfolio, the track record of its management team, and the prevailing market conditions before making investment decisions.

15.5 How to Invest in REITs

When it comes to investing in REITs, there are several important considerations to keep in mind. This section explores the various options available for REIT investments, how to evaluate the performance of REITs, the considerations for choosing REITs, where to invest in REITs and the importance of monitoring and reviewing REIT investments.By following these guidelines, investors can navigate the REIT market and make informed investment decisions.

Investing in REITs can be done through various options and requires careful evaluation. Here are the steps to invest in REITs:

1. **Understanding REIT Investment Options:** There are different types of REITs available for investment. *Publicly traded REITs* are listed on stock exchanges and can be bought and sold like any other publicly traded stock. *Non-traded REITs* are not listed on stock exchanges and typically have limited liquidity. *Exchange-traded funds (ETFs)* that focus on REITs provide a diversified investment option.

2. **Evaluating REIT Performance:** Before investing in a REIT, conduct a thorough financial analysis of the company. Review its *financial statements*, including revenue, net operating income, and funds from operations. Pay attention to metrics such as *dividend yield*, which indicates the annual dividend payout relative to the share price. Also, consider the *total return of the REIT*, which combines dividends and capital appreciation.

3. **Considerations for Choosing REITs:** Take into account the sector focus of the REIT. Some REITs specialize in specific *property sectors* like residential, healthcare, retail, or industrial. Assess the *management team's experience* and track record in managing REITs and their ability to execute the investment strategy effectively. Research the *REIT's historical performance*, including its dividend history and total returns.

4. **Investing in REITs through Brokerage Accounts, Retirement Accounts, or REIT Funds:** REITs can be purchased through *brokerage accounts*, where investors can buy and sell shares of publicly traded REITs like individual stocks. Additionally, REITs can be included in *retirement accounts* such as IRAs or 401(k)s, offering potential tax advantages. Another option is *investing in REIT funds*, which

are managed portfolios of various REITs that provide diversification.

5. **Importance of Regular Monitoring and Review:** Once invested in REITs, it's crucial to regularly monitor the performance of the REITs in your portfolio. Stay informed about *market and economic conditions* that may impact the performance of the REITs. Review the *financial reports and disclosures* provided by the REITs to ensure they continue to meet your investment objectives. Consider *re-evaluating your portfolio* periodically and make adjustments as necessary.

It's recommended to consult with a financial advisor who specializes in real estate investments or a qualified professional to help guide your investment decisions and ensure they align with your financial goals and risk tolerance.

Conclusion

In conclusion, understanding real estate investment trusts (REITs) is crucial for investors interested in private equity real estate. REITs provide access to the commercial real estate market and offer benefits such as diversification, access to professional management, and the potential for regular income and capital appreciation. However, thorough research and due diligence are essential when investing in REITs. Evaluating financial performance, considering dividend yield and total return, and assessing sector focus and management track record are important factors to consider. Regular monitoring and staying informed about market conditions are also vital. Subsequent chapters will delve deeper into specific aspects of REIT investments, providing further insights into this investment vehicle.

Chapter 16: Tax Considerations for Private Equity Real Estate Investing

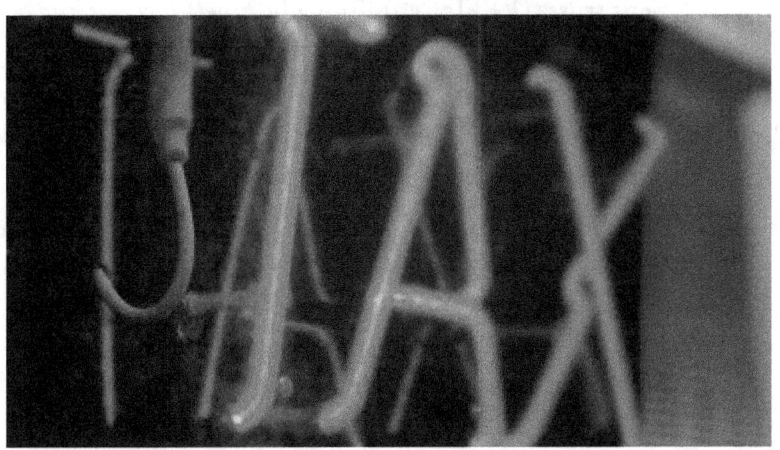

Tax - Photo by Jon Tyson

16.1 Overview of Tax Considerations for Private Equity Real Estate Investing

This section emphasizes the importance of understanding tax implications in private equity real estate investing to maximize profitability. It covers key considerations such as income taxes, capital gains taxes, property taxes, tax-deferred exchanges, and depreciation benefits. Timing property dispositions and seeking guidance from a tax professional are recommended for effective tax planning. Managing tax implications is crucial for success in private equity real estate investments.

Here is an overview of the key tax aspects to consider:

1. **Income Taxes:** Income generated from private equity real

estate investments is generally subject to income tax. The tax treatment can vary depending on the structure of the investment and the tax laws of the jurisdiction. It's important to understand the *tax rates* applicable to rental income, partnership income, or distributions from real estate investment trusts (REITs). Additionally, *tax deductions and credits related to expenses* incurred in property management and operations should be taken into account.

2. **Capital Gains Taxes:** When selling a real estate investment, capital gains taxes may apply on the profit earned. The tax rate for capital gains depends on the holding period of the investment and the tax laws in the respective jurisdiction. *Short-term capital gains*, realized on investments held for less than a year, are typically taxed at higher rates compared to *long-term capital gains*, which are applicable for investments held for over a year. Proper tax planning can help optimize the timing of property dispositions to minimize the tax burden.

3. **Property Taxes:** Real estate investments are subject to property taxes imposed by local governments. These taxes are *based on the assessed value* of the property and can vary depending on the location. It's important to consider property taxes when evaluating the cash flow and overall profitability of an investment property.

Apart from these key tax considerations, other factors such as **tax-deferred exchanges** (e.g., 1031 exchanges in the United States), tax benefits related to **depreciation and amortization**, and tax implications of **financing arrangements** should also be taken into account.

Tax laws and regulations are subject to change, so it's crucial to stay updated on any new developments that may impact private equity real estate investments.

Given the complexity of tax matters, **consulting with a qualified tax professional** who specializes in real estate investments is highly recommended. They can provide tailored advice and help navigate the intricacies of tax planning, ensuring compliance with tax laws while optimizing tax efficiency. Understanding and properly managing tax implications is an integral part of successful private equity real estate investing.

Effectively managing tax implications is integral to achieving success in private equity real estate investing. Understanding the tax implications is crucial in private equity real estate investing as it directly impacts profitability. This section provides an overview of key tax considerations and emphasizes the importance of understanding tax rates. Proper tax planning is highlighted and additional factors should also be considered.

16.2 Tax Implications of Different Types of Private Equity Real Estate Investments

The tax implications of private equity real estate investments can have a significant impact on the overall financial outcome. This section provides an overview of the tax considerations for different types of private equity real estate investments. It's crucial to stay informed about changing tax laws and consult with a tax professional specializing in real estate investments for accurate tax planning and compliance.

The tax implications of private equity real estate investments can vary depending on the type of investment. Here's an overview of the tax considerations for different types of private equity real estate investments:

1. **Residential Real Estate Investments:** Income generated from residential real estate investments, such as rental properties or multifamily buildings, is generally subject to *income tax*. Rental income is typically treated as ordinary income and taxed at the applicable income tax rates. However, certain tax deductions and credits may be available, including deductions for mortgage interest, property taxes, repairs and maintenance expenses, and depreciation. It's important to comply with local regulations and tax laws regarding residential rental properties.

2. **Commercial and Industrial Real Estate Investments:** Tax considerations for commercial and industrial real estate investments are similar to residential properties. Rental income is subject to *income tax*, and expenses related to property management, maintenance, and depreciation can be deducted. Additionally, commercial properties may have unique tax implications, such as *tenant improvements and build-to-suit considerations*. It's essential to consult with a tax professional to understand the specific tax rules and regulations related to commercial and industrial real estate investments.

3. **Specialized Real Estate:** Investments in specialized real estate sectors like *hospitality* (hotels, resorts), *healthcare* (medical facilities, senior housing), and others can have specific tax implications. These sectors may have additional tax considerations, such as *revenue recognition rules*, healthcare industry regulations, or tax benefits related to the operation of certain types of facilities. Understanding the unique tax landscape of specialized real estate sectors is crucial for accurate tax planning and compliance.

4. **Real Estate Investment Trusts (REITs):** REITs offer certain tax advantages and are subject to specific tax regulations. To

qualify as a REIT, the entity must distribute a significant portion of its taxable income to shareholders. REIT distributions are generally taxed as *ordinary income* for shareholders. However, shareholders may benefit from the *qualified dividend tax rate* if certain criteria are met. REITs themselves are generally *not subject to federal income tax* at the corporate level, provided they distribute a certain percentage of income to shareholders and meet other requirements. REIT taxation rules may vary by jurisdiction, so it's important to understand the specific tax regulations applicable to REITs.

It's worth noting that tax laws and regulations are complex and subject to change. The tax implications of private equity real estate investments can be influenced by various factors, including the entity structure, investment holding period, financing arrangements, and jurisdiction-specific tax rules. To ensure compliance and optimize tax efficiency, consulting with a tax professional experienced in real estate investments is highly recommended. They can provide tailored guidance based on your specific investment objectives and circumstances.

16.3 How to Minimize Tax Liabilities in Private Equity Real Estate Investing

Minimizing tax liabilities is a key objective in private equity real estate investing. This section explores various strategies to achieve this goal. Effective tax planning involves making informed decisions regarding entity selection and capital structure. Additionally, utilizing tax-advantaged investment vehicles like 1031 exchanges and Opportunity Zones can provide significant tax benefits. Depreciation and cost segregation strategies help optimize deductions, while identifying deductible expenses and leveraging tax credits further reduces tax burdens. By implementing these techniques, investors can strategically minimize tax liabilities and enhance their returns in private equity real estate investing.

Minimizing tax liabilities is a key objective in private equity real estate investing. Here are some strategies to consider for effective tax planning:

1. **Entity Selection and Capital Structure:** Choosing the right entity structure for your real estate investments can have significant tax implications. Options include *partnerships, limited liability companies (LLCs),* or *corporations.* Each entity type has its own tax treatment, so it's important to evaluate the pros and cons and select the structure that aligns with your investment goals. Additionally, optimizing the *capital structure by balancing debt and equity* can help maximize tax advantages, such as interest expense deductions.
2. **Utilizing Tax-Advantaged Investment Vehicles:**
    1. *1031 Exchanges:* A 1031 exchange allows for the *deferral of capital gains taxes* on the sale of a property if the proceeds are reinvested in a like-kind property. By reinvesting in a qualifying property, investors can defer taxes and potentially accumulate wealth through property exchanges.
    2. *Opportunity Zones:* Opportunity Zones provide tax incentives for investing in designated *economically distressed areas.* By investing capital gains in qualified opportunity zone funds, investors can defer and potentially reduce capital gains taxes on their original investment.
3. **Depreciation and Cost Segregation Strategies:** Real estate investments can benefit from depreciation deductions. Cost segregation is a strategy that involves identifying and

reclassifying components of a property to *accelerate depreciation* deductions. This can help generate greater tax deductions in the early years of ownership, improving cash flow and reducing tax liabilities.

4. **Deductible Expenses and Tax Credits:** Properly tracking and deducting eligible expenses is crucial for *minimizing tax liabilities*. Deductible expenses may include property management fees, repairs and maintenance costs, property taxes, insurance premiums, and professional fees. Additionally, certain *tax credits*, such as energy efficiency credits or historic rehabilitation credits, can provide further tax benefits.

It's important to note that tax planning should be done in consultation with a qualified tax professional who is knowledgeable about real estate investments. They can help navigate the complex tax landscape, ensure compliance with tax laws, and identify opportunities to minimize tax liabilities based on your specific investment structure and objectives. Regular review and adjustment of tax strategies as tax laws evolve is also crucial to optimize tax efficiency in private equity real estate investing.

16.4 Tax Pitfalls to Avoid in Private Equity Real Estate Investing

Tax risks must be minimized and compliance ensured in private equity real estate investing. This section offers strategies to avoid tax pitfalls. Understanding compliance requirements, identifying and addressing potential traps, and assessing the impact of tax law changes are crucial. Mitigating audit and penalty risks involves maintaining accurate records, conducting internal audits, and seeking professional advice. By navigating these pitfalls, investors can safeguard their investments and optimize outcomes in private equity real estate.

While minimizing tax liabilities is important in private equity real estate investing, it is equally crucial to avoid tax pitfalls. Here are some common tax pitfalls to be aware of and steps to mitigate them:

1. **Understanding Tax Compliance Requirements:** Private equity real estate investors must have a clear understanding of *tax compliance obligations*. This includes *filing accurate tax returns, reporting income and expenses correctly*, and *adhering to deadlines*. Failure to meet compliance requirements can lead to *penalties* and *audits*.

2. **Identifying and Addressing Potential Tax Traps:** Real estate transactions involve *complex tax rules and regulations*. It is essential to identify potential tax traps and seek professional advice to address them appropriately. Examples include properly structuring deals involving partnerships, ensuring compliance with passive activity loss rules, and understanding the tax consequences of debt restructuring.

3. **Assessing the Impact of Tax Law Changes and Regulatory Updates:** Tax laws and regulations are subject to change, and new legislation can have significant implications for private equity real estate investors. Staying informed about tax law updates and assessing their impact on your investments is crucial. *Engaging with tax professionals* who specialize in real estate can help navigate these changes and implement appropriate strategies.

4. **Mitigating Risks of Tax Audits and Penalties:** Tax audits can be time-consuming, costly, and disruptive to business operations. To mitigate the risk of audits and penalties, it is essential to *maintain accurate and detailed records, ensure consistency in reporting* across different entities, and *conduct periodic reviews* to identify and rectify any potential red flags. Engaging with experienced tax professionals can provide

valuable guidance and support in maintaining compliance and minimizing audit risks.

5. **Ongoing Tax Planning and Monitoring:** Tax planning should be an ongoing process, taking into account *changes in tax laws, investment strategies*, and *personal circumstances*. Regular monitoring and adjustment of tax strategies can help identify and *address potential tax pitfalls* and *optimize tax efficiency* in private equity real estate investing.

It is recommended to work closely with qualified tax professionals who specialize in real estate taxation to ensure compliance, mitigate risks, and optimize tax strategies based on your specific investment goals and circumstances. By proactively addressing tax pitfalls, investors can navigate the tax landscape more effectively and protect their investments.

16.5 Case Studies of Successful and Unsuccessful Tax Strategies

This section examines two case studies that illustrate the impact of tax planning on private equity real estate investing. Learning from these tax mistakes and failures is crucial for investors to implement sound tax planning strategies, seek professional advice, and conduct thorough due diligence. Analyzing the impact of tax planning on investment returns and learning from both successful and unsuccessful tax strategies can provide valuable insights for private equity real estate investors.

Case Study 1: Successful Tax Strategy

In this case study, a private equity real estate investor successfully implemented a tax strategy to maximize investment returns. The investor utilized a 1031 exchange, which allows for the deferral of capital gains taxes by reinvesting the proceeds from the sale of one property into the purchase of another like-kind property. By utilizing this strategy, the investor was able to defer the recognition of capital gains taxes, effectively increasing the amount available for reinvestment. This tax deferral provided a significant boost to the investor's overall return on investment.

Case Study 2: Unsuccessful Tax Strategy

In this case study, a private equity real estate investor failed to properly plan for tax consequences, resulting in a significant tax liability and reduced investment returns. The investor acquired a commercial property with a large mortgage, intending to claim substantial depreciation deductions to offset rental income. However, due to inadequate record-keeping and failure to meet the requirements for active participation in real estate activities, the investor was deemed a passive investor by the tax authorities. As a result, the depreciation deductions were disallowed, leading to a higher tax liability and lower investment returns than anticipated.

Learning from Tax Mistakes and Failures

Learning from tax mistakes and failures is essential for private equity real estate investors. It highlights the importance of conducting thorough due diligence, seeking professional tax advice, and implementing sound tax planning strategies. By studying real-life examples of tax pitfalls and failures, investors can understand the potential consequences of inadequate tax planning and make informed decisions to avoid similar mistakes.

Analyzing the impact of tax planning on investment returns and learning from both successful and unsuccessful tax strategies can provide valuable insights for private equity real estate investors. It emphasizes the significance of proactive tax planning, professional guidance, and ongoing monitoring to optimize tax efficiency and maximize investment returns.

Conclusion

In conclusion, tax considerations play a vital role in private equity real estate investing. Understanding the tax implications of different investment types, such as residential, commercial, and specialized real estate, is essential for making informed decisions. By leveraging tax-advantaged investment vehicles and implementing effective tax planning strategies, investors can minimize tax liabilities and maximize their investment returns. Consulting with tax professionals and legal counsel is highly recommended to navigate the complex tax landscape and ensure compliance with tax regulations.

About The Author

JIM PELLERIN started real estate investing over twenty years ago. Since then, he has bought and sold millions of dollars of real estate. He began by purchasing and renting out duplexes. Following that he added Lease Options to his strategy. He has implemented many creative funding strategies that have allowed him to continue implementing various strategies and alloqed him to build a sizable portfolio.

As part of his education, he has attended numerous seminars on real estate investing, project management, property management, financing, renovations, motivation, time management, and many more. He has also read over 500 books on similar topics.

This book blends his experience and the knowledge he has gained through his investments and studies.

Visit his author page to discover my other publications: books2read.com/JimPellerin[1]

---

1. https://books2read.com/JimPellerin

Other Books By Jim Pellerin

Real Estate Investing: Strategies – The Secret to Financial Independence with Real Estate

books2read.com/strategies[1]

1. https://books2read.com/strategies

Real Estate Investing with Lease Options – How to Invest with No Money Down

books2read.com/Lease-Options[2]

---

2. https://books2read.com/Lease-Options

Invest NOW – The Passive Approach to Winning with Real Estate

books2read.com/investnow[3]

---

3. https://books2read.com/investnow

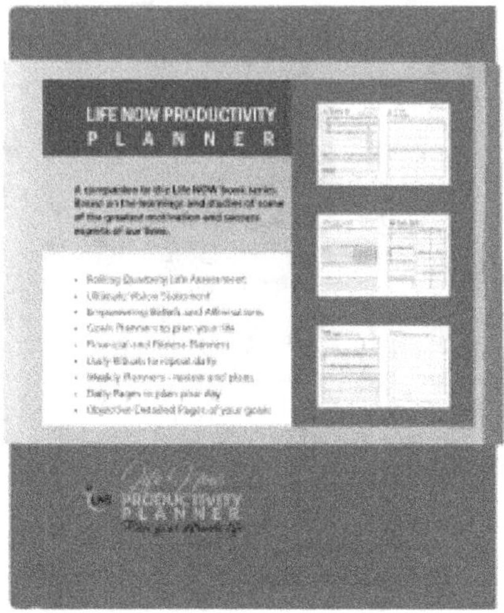

books2read.com/JimPellerin[4]

---

4. https://books2read.com/JimPellerin

Don't miss out!

Visit the website below and you can sign up to receive emails whenever Jim Pellerin publishes a new book. There's no charge and no obligation.

https://books2read.com/r/B-A-WGIX-RGBJC

BOOKS2READ

Connecting independent readers to independent writers.

Did you love *The Ultimate Beginners Guide to Private Equity Real Estate Investing*? Then you should read *Real Estate Investing Strategies: The Secret to Financial Independence with Real Estate*[5] by Jim Pellerin!

The mechanics of Real Estate Investing is simple: Buy a house and do something with it. Fix it and rent it, or just sell it. Sounds simple, doesn't it? Yet only a small percentage of us have enough courage to go out and take advantage of the opportunities that are available to us. Real Estate Investing can be more promising than stocks, bonds, and various other securities because of the higher rates of return.

In this book, I show you how to get started by describing the different types of skills you need, by showing you how to take control of your personal and financial situation, and by helping you decide what type of real estate investing you want to get involved in. I also show

---

5. https://books2read.com/u/m2QyNG

6. https://books2read.com/u/m2QyNG

you how to find properties, how to analyze them, and how to make an offer that makes sense. And finally, I describe what you need to do to manage your investment and ultimately how to sell your investment for the most profit.

I have been involved in real estate investing for over 20 years. I have yet to find a book that focuses on the investor and the overall process. Sure, there are lots of books on fix and flips, buy, rent and hold, rent to own, etc. However, I haven't found any good books on how to really get started in the real estate investing process from a practical viewpoint. The technical aspects of real estate investing are really quite easy. But if it's so easy, then why isn't everyone doing it?

This book is for people who are serious about getting started in real estate investing and who want to join the 5% of those who actually take action and invest. This book provides a strategic approach with the tried and tested methods and principles that have helped others make millions in real estate.

Read more at www.jimpellerin.com.

Also by Jim Pellerin

Real Estate Investing
Real Estate Investing Strategies: The Secret to Financial Independence with Real Estate
Real Estate Investing with Lease Options - Investing in Real Estate with No Money Down
Invest Now - The Passive Approach to Winning at Real Estate
The Ultimate Beginners Guide to Real Estate Investing
The 98 Best Real Estate Investing Strategies
The Ultimate Beginners Guide to Wholesale Real Estate Investing
The Ultimate Beginners Guide to Rental Real Estate Investing
The Ultimate Beginners Guide to Fix and Flip Real Estate Investing
The Ultimate Beginners Guide to Private Equity Real Estate Investing

Watch for more at www.jimpellerin.com.

9 798223 688594